KU-521-392

COLLINS
GEM

FRENCH
GRAMMAR

Lesley A. Robertson M.A.
Lorna A. Sinclair B.A., Ph.D.

HarperCollins*Publishers*

first published 1984

© William Collins Sons & Co. Ltd. 1984

latest reprint 1992

ISBN 0 00 459334 0

Series Editor
Richard H. Thomas

*Printed in Great Britain by
HarperCollins Manufacturing, Glasgow*

If your knowledge of French grammar is elementary, non-existent or just rusty, this book has been designed to help you to get to grips with the basic features of the French language. Those with a more advanced grasp of French will find it an invaluable guide for reference and revision.

You will see from the list of contents overleaf that the text has been divided according to parts of speech (nouns, adjectives, verbs etc.). We've tried to anticipate those grammatical terms with which you might not be familiar, and a brief explanation (or illustration) is often provided at a relevant point in the text. A special feature of this book is the clear demarcation of grammatical points, illustrated by numerous examples. For instance, if you turn to page 30, you'll see a series of bracketed numbers, $(\rightarrow 1)$ to $(\rightarrow 7)$, throughout the page. These numbers cross-refer you to an example, or group of examples, on page 31. In this way, individual grammatical points given on the left-hand page are illustrated on the right-hand page. This means that the examples are readily accessible to the learner without obscuring the clarity of presentation.

Throughout the book, special attention has been paid to areas in which French usage differs from English usage, particularly in the section on sentence structure. Other sections include: use of numbers, translation problems and pronunciation. The translation problem section alerts you to some of the pitfalls of translation, and provides a selection of frequently recurring problems, showing how to solve them. A fully comprehensive index, containing key words in both French and English, as well as subject references, completes the grammar.

Abbreviations used

ctd.	continued	p(p).	page(s)	qn	quelqu'un
fem.	feminine	perf.	perfect	sb	somebody
infin.	infinitive	plur.	plural	sing.	singular
masc.	masculine	qch	quelque chose	sth	something

4 CONTENTS

Simple Tenses: formation

In French the simple tenses are:

Present	(→1)
Imperfect	(→2)
Future	(→3)
Conditional	(→4)
Past Historic	(→5)
Present Subjunctive	(→6)
Imperfect Subjunctive	(→7)

They are formed by adding endings to a verb stem. The endings show the number and person of the subject of the verb (→8)

The stem and endings of regular verbs are totally predictable. The following sections show all the patterns for regular verbs. For irregular verbs see pp. 74 ff.

Regular Verbs

There are three regular verb patterns (called conjugations), each identifiable by the ending of the infinitive:

- First conjugation verbs end in **-er** e.g. **donner** to give

- Second conjugation verbs end in **-ir** e.g. **finir** to finish

- Third conjugation verbs end in **-re** e.g. **vendre** to sell

These three conjugations are treated in order on the following pages.

Continued

1 je donne
I give, I am giving, I do give

2 je donnais
I gave, I was giving, I used to give

3 je donnerai
I shall give, I shall be giving

4 je donnerais
I should/would give, I should/would be giving

5 je donnai
I gave

6 (que) je donne
(that) I give/gave

7 (que) je donnasse
(that) I gave

8 je donne	I give
nous donnons	we give
je donnerais	I would give
nous donnerions	we would give

Simple Tenses: First Conjugation

- The stem is formed as follows:

TENSE	FORMATION	EXAMPLE
Present		
Imperfect		
Past Historic	} infinitive minus **-er**	**donn-**
Present Subjunctive		
Imperfect Subjunctive		
Future	} infinitive	**donner-**
Conditional		

- To the appropriate stem add the following endings:

		PRESENT (→1)	IMPERFECT (→2)	PAST HISTORIC (→3)
sing.	1st person	-e	-ais	-ai
	2nd person	-es	-ais	-as
	3rd person	-e	-ait	-a
plur.	1st person	-ons	-ions	-âmes
	2nd person	-ez	-iez	-âtes
	3rd person	-ent	-aient	-èrent

		PRESENT SUBJUNCTIVE (→4)	IMPERFECT SUBJUNCTIVE (→5)
sing.	1st person	-e	-asse
	2nd person	-es	-asses
	3rd person	-e	-ât
plur.	1st person	-ions	-assions
	2nd person	-iez	-assiez
	3rd person	-ent	-assent

		FUTURE (→6)	CONDITIONAL (→7)
sing.	1st person	-ai	-ais
	2nd person	-as	-ais
	3rd person	-a	-ait
plur.	1st person	-ons	-ions
	2nd person	-ez	-iez
	3rd person	-ont	-aient

1 PRESENT

je donne
tu donnes
il donne
elle donne
nous donnons
vous donnez
ils donnent
elles donnent

2 IMPERFECT

je donnais
tu donnais
il donnait
elle donnait
nous donnions
vous donniez
ils donnaient
elles donnaient

3 PAST HISTORIC

je donnai
tu donnas
il donna
elle donna
nous donnâmes
vous donnâtes
ils donnèrent
elles donnèrent

4 PRESENT SUBJUNCTIVE

je donne
tu donnes
il donne
elle donne
nous donnions
vous donniez
ils donnent
elles donnent

5 IMPERFECT SUBJUNCTIVE

je donnasse
tu donnasses
il donnât
elle donnât
nous donnassions
vous donnassiez
ils donnassent
elles donnassent

6 FUTURE

je donnerai
tu donneras
il donnera
elle donnera
nous donnerons
vous donnerez
ils donneront
elles donneront

7 CONDITIONAL

je donnerais
tu donnerais
il donnerait
elle donnerait
nous donnerions
vous donneriez
ils donneraient
elles donneraient

Simple Tenses: Second Conjugation

● The stem is formed as follows:

TENSE	FORMATION	EXAMPLE
Present		
Imperfect		
Past Historic	infinitive minus **-ir**	**fin-**
Present Subjunctive		
Imperfect Subjunctive		
Future	infinitive	**finir-**
Conditional		

● To the appropriate stem add the following endings:

		PRESENT (→1)	IMPERFECT (→2)	PAST HISTORIC (→3)
sing.	1st person	-is	-issais	-is
	2nd person	-is	-issais	-is
	3rd person	-it	-issait	-it
plur.	1st person	-issons	-issions	-îmes
	2nd person	-issez	-issiez	-îtes
	3rd person	-issent	-issaient	-irent

		PRESENT SUBJUNCTIVE (→4)	IMPERFECT SUBJUNCTIVE (→5)
sing.	1st person	-isse	-isse
	2nd person	-isses	-isses
	3rd person	-isse	-ît
plur.	1st person	-issions	-issions
	2nd person	-issiez	-issiez
	3rd person	-issent	-issent

		FUTURE (→6)	CONDITIONAL (→7)
sing.	1st person	-ai	-ais
	2nd person	-as	-ais
	3rd person	-a	-ait
plur.	1st person	-ons	-ions
	2nd person	-ez	-iez
	3rd person	-ont	-aient

1 PRESENT

je fin**is**
tu fin**is**
il fin**it**
elle fin**it**
nous fin**issons**
vous fin**issez**
ils fin**issent**
elles fin**issent**

2 IMPERFECT

je fin**issais**
tu fin**issais**
il fin**issait**
elle fin**issait**
nous fin**issions**
vous fin**issiez**
ils fin**issaient**
elles fin**issaient**

3 PAST HISTORIC

je fin**is**
tu fin**is**
il fin**it**
elle fin**it**
nous fin**îmes**
vous fin**îtes**
ils fin**irent**
elles fin**irent**

4 PRESENT SUBJUNCTIVE

je fin**isse**
tu fin**isses**
il fin**isse**
elle fin**isse**
nous fin**issions**
vous fin**issiez**
ils fin**issent**
elles fin**issent**

5 IMPERFECT SUBJUNCTIVE

je fin**isse**
tu fin**isses**
il fin**ît**
elle fin**ît**
nous fin**issions**
vous fin**issiez**
ils fin**issent**
elles fin**issent**

6 FUTURE

je fin**irai**
tu fin**iras**
il fin**ira**
elle fin**ira**
nous fin**irons**
vous fin**irez**
ils fin**iront**
elles fin**iront**

7 CONDITIONAL

je fin**irais**
tu fin**irais**
il fin**irait**
elle fin**irait**
nous fin**irions**
vous fin**iriez**
ils fin**iraient**
elles fin**iraient**

Simple Tenses: Third Conjugation

● The stem is formed as follows:

TENSE	FORMATION	EXAMPLE
Present		
Imperfect		
Past Historic	infinitive minus **-re**	**vend-**
Present Subjunctive		
Imperfect Subjunctive		
Future	infinitive minus **-e**	**vendr-**
Conditional		

● To the appropriate stem add the following endings:

		PRESENT (→1)	IMPERFECT (→2)	PAST HISTORIC (→3)
sing.	1st person	-s	-ais	-is
	2nd person	-s	-ais	-is
	3rd person	–	-ait	-it
plur.	1st person	-ons	-ions	-îmes
	2nd person	-ez	-iez	-îtes
	3rd person	-ent	-aient	-irent

		PRESENT SUBJUNCTIVE (→4)	IMPERFECT SUBJUNCTIVE (→5)
sing.	1st person	-e	-isse
	2nd person	-es	-isses
	3rd person	-e	-ît
plur.	1st person	-ions	-issions
	2nd person	-iez	-issiez
	3rd person	-ent	-issent

		FUTURE (→6)	CONDITIONAL (→7)
sing.	1st person	-ai	-ais
	2nd person	-as	-ais
	3rd person	-a	-ait
plur.	1st person	-ons	-ions
	2nd person	-ez	-iez
	3rd person	-ont	-aient

1 PRESENT	**2** IMPERFECT	**3** PAST HISTORIC
je vend**s**	je vend**ais**	je vend**is**
tu vend**s**	tu vend**ais**	tu vend**is**
il vend	il vend**ait**	il vend**it**
elle vend	elle vend**ait**	elle vend**it**
nous vend**ons**	nous vend**ions**	nous vend**îmes**
vous vend**ez**	vous vend**iez**	vous vend**îtes**
ils vend**ent**	ils vend**aient**	ils vend**irent**
elles vend**ent**	elles vend**aient**	elles vend**irent**

4 PRESENT SUBJUNCTIVE	**5** IMPERFECT SUBJUNCTIVE
je vend**e**	je vend**isse**
tu vend**es**	tu vend**isses**
il vend**e**	il vend**ît**
elle vend**e**	elle vend**ît**
nous vend**ions**	nous vend**issions**
vous vend**iez**	vous vend**issiez**
ils vend**ent**	ils vend**issent**
elles vend**ent**	elles vend**issent**

6 FUTURE	**7** CONDITIONAL
je vend**rai**	je vend**rais**
tu vend**ras**	tu vend**rais**
il vend**ra**	il vend**rait**
elle vend**ra**	elle vend**rait**
nous vend**rons**	nous vend**rions**
vous vend**rez**	vous vend**riez**
ils vend**ront**	ils vend**raient**
elles vend**ront**	elles vend**raient**

1st Conjugation Spelling Irregularities

Before certain endings, the stems of some '-er' verbs may change
slightly.

Below, and on subsequent pages, the verb types are identified, and
the changes described are illustrated by means of a representative
verb.

Verbs ending:	**-cer**
Change:	**c** becomes **ç** before **a** or **o**
Tenses affected:	Present, Imperfect, Past Historic, Imperfect Subjunctive, Present Participle
Model:	**lancer** *to throw* (→1)

- Why the change occurs:
  A cedilla is added to the **c** to retain its soft [s] pronunciation
  before the vowels **a** and **o**

Verbs ending:	**-ger**
Change:	**g** becomes **ge** before **a** or **o**
Tenses affected:	Present, Imperfect, Past Historic, Imperfect Subjunctive, Present Participle
Model:	**manger** *to eat* (→2)

- Why the change occurs:
  An **e** is added after the **g** to retain its soft [ʒ] pronunciation before
  the vowels **a** and **o**

Continued

1 INFINITIVE
lancer

PRESENT PARTICIPLE
lançant

PRESENT
je lance
tu lances
il/elle lance
nous lançons
vous lancez
ils/elles lancent

IMPERFECT
je lançais
tu lançais
il/elle lançait
nous lancions
vous lanciez
ils/elles lançaient

PAST HISTORIC
je lançai
tu lanças
il/elle lança
nous lançâmes
vous lançâtes
ils/elles lancèrent

IMPERFECT SUBJUNCTIVE
je lançasse
tu lançasses
il/elle lançât
nous lançassions
vous lançassiez
ils/elles lançassent

2 INFINITIVE
manger

PRESENT PARTICIPLE
mangeant

PRESENT
je mange
tu manges
il/elle mange
nous mangeons
vous mangez
ils/elles mangent

IMPERFECT
je mangeais
tu mangeais
il/elle mangeait
nous mangions
vous mangiez
ils/elles mangeaient

PAST HISTORIC
je mangeai
tu mangeas
il/elle mangea
nous mangeâmes
vous mangeâtes
ils/elles mangèrent

IMPERFECT SUBJUNCTIVE
je mangeasse
tu mangeasses
il/elle mangeât
nous mangeassions
vous mangeassiez
ils/elles mangeassent

1st Conjugation Spelling Irregularities (ctd.)

Verbs ending	**-eler**
Change:	**-l** doubles before **-e, -es, -ent** and throughout the Future and Conditional tenses
Tenses affected:	Present, Present Subjunctive, Future, Conditional
Model:	**appeler** *to call* (→**1**)

- Exceptions: **geler** *to freeze* } like **mener** (p. 18)
  peler *to peel*

Verbs ending	**-eter**
Change:	**-t** doubles before **-e, -es, -ent** and throughout the Future and Conditional tenses
Tenses affected:	Present, Present Subjunctive, Future, Conditional
Model:	**jeter** *to throw* (→**2**)

- Exceptions: **acheter** *to buy* } like **mener** (p. 18)
  haleter *to pant*

Verbs ending	**-yer**
Change:	**y** changes to **i** before **-e, -es, -ent** and throughout the Future and Conditional tenses
Tenses affected:	Present, Present Subjunctive, Future, Conditional
Model:	**essuyer** *to wipe* (→**3**)

- The change described is optional for verbs ending in **-ayer** e.g. **payer** *to pay*, **essayer** *to try*

Continued

1 PRESENT (+ SUBJUNCTIVE)

j'appelle
tu appelles
il/elle appelle
nous appelons
  (appelions)
vous appelez
  (appeliez)
ils/elles appellent

FUTURE

j'appellerai
tu appelleras
il appellera *etc.*

CONDITIONAL

j'appellerais
tu appellerais
il appellerait *etc.*

2 PRESENT (+ SUBJUNCTIVE)

je jette
tu jettes
il/elle jette
nous jetons
  (jetions)
vous jetez
  (jetiez)
ils/elles jettent

FUTURE

je jetterai
tu jetteras
il jettera *etc.*

CONDITIONAL

je jetterais
tu jetterais
il jetterait *etc.*

3 PRESENT (+ SUBJUNCTIVE)

j'essuie
tu essuies
il/elle essuie
nous essuyons
  (essuyions)
vous essuyez
  (essuyiez)
ils/elles essuient

FUTURE

j'essuierai
tu essuieras
il essuiera *etc.*

CONDITIONAL

j'essuierais
tu essuierais
il essuierait *etc.*

1st Conjugation Spelling Irregularities (ctd.)

Verbs like:	**mener, peser, lever** etc
Change:	e changes to è before **-e, -es, -ent** and throughout the Future and Conditional tenses
Tenses affected:	Present, Present Subjunctive, Future, Conditional
Model:	**mener** *to lead* (→**1**)

Verbs like:	**céder, régler, espérer** etc
Change:	é changes to è before **-e, -es, -ent**
Tenses affected:	Present, Present Subjunctive
Model:	**céder** *to yield* (→**2**)

1 PRESENT (+ SUBJUNCTIVE)   FUTURE

je **mène**	je **mènerai**
tu **mènes**	tu **mèneras**
il/elle **mène**	il **mènera** *etc.*
nous menons	
(menions)	CONDITIONAL
vous menez	je **mènerais**
(meniez)	tu **mènerais**
ils/elles **mènent**	il **mènerait** *etc.*

2 PRESENT (+ SUBJUNCTIVE)

je **cède**
tu **cèdes**
il/elle **cède**
nous cédons
(cédions)
vous cédez
(cédiez)
ils/elles **cèdent**

20 VERBS

The Imperative

The imperative is the form of the verb used to give commands or orders. It can be used politely, as in English 'Shut the door, please'.

The imperative is the same as the present tense **tu**, **nous** and **vous** forms without the subject pronouns:

donne*	**finis**	**vends**
give	*finish*	*sell*

*The final 's' of the present tense of 1st conjugation verbs is dropped, except before **y** and **en** (→**1**)

donnons	**finissons**	**vendons**
let's give	*let's finish*	*let's sell*

donnez	**finissez**	**vendez**
give	*finish*	*sell*

● The imperative of irregular verbs is given in the verb tables pp. 74 ff.

● Position of object pronouns with the imperative:
  in POSITIVE commands: they follow the verb and are attached to it by hyphens (→**2**)
  in NEGATIVE commands: they precede the verb and are not attached to it (→**3**)

● For the order of object pronouns, see page 170

● For reflexive verbs – e.g. **se lever** *to get up* – the object pronoun is the reflexive pronoun (→**4**)

1 Compare: **Tu donnes de l'argent à Paul**
You give (some) money to Paul
and: **Donne de l'argent à Paul**
Give (some) money to Paul

2 **Excusez-moi**
Excuse me
Choisis-nous
Choose us
Attendons-la
Let's wait for her/it

Envoyons-les-leur
Let's send them to them
Expliquez-le-moi
Explain it to me
Rends-la-lui
Give it back to him/her

3 **Ne me dérange pas**
Don't disturb me
Ne les punissons pas
Let's not punish them
Ne leur répondez pas
Don't answer them

Ne leur en parlons pas
Let's not speak to them about it
N'y réfléchis plus
Don't think about it any more
Ne la lui rendons pas
Let's not give it back to him/her

4 **Lève-toi**
Get up
Levons-nous
Let's get up
Levez-vous
Get up

Ne te lève pas
Don't get up
Ne nous levons pas
Let's not get up
Ne vous levez pas
Don't get up

Compound Tenses: formation

In French the compound tenses are:

Perfect	(→1)
Pluperfect	(→2)
Future Perfect	(→3)
Conditional Perfect	(→4)
Past Anterior	(→5)
Perfect Subjunctive	(→6)
Pluperfect Subjunctive	(→7)

They consist of the past participle of the verb together with an auxiliary verb. Most verbs take the auxiliary **avoir**, but some take **être** (see p. 28).

Compound tenses are formed in exactly the same way for both regular and irregular verbs, the only difference being that irregular verbs may have an irregular past participle.

The Past Participle

For all compound tenses you need to know how to form the past participle of the verb. For regular verbs this is as follows:

- 1st conjugation: replace the **-er** of the infinitive by **-é** (→8)
- 2nd conjugation: replace the **-ir** of the infinitive by **-i** (→9)
- 3rd conjugation: replace the **-re** of the infinitive by **-u** (→10)

- See p. 50 for agreement of past participles.

Continued

with **avoir**	with **être**
1 j'ai donné I gave, have given	je suis tombé I fell, have fallen
2 j'avais donné I had given	j'étais tombé I had fallen
3 j'aurai donné I shall have given	je serai tombé I shall have fallen
4 j'aurais donné I should/would have given	je serais tombé I should/would have fallen
5 j'eus donné I had given	je fus tombé I had fallen
6 (que) j'aie donné (that) I gave, have given	(que) je sois tombé (that) I fell, have fallen
7 (que) j'eusse donné (that) I had given	(que) je fusse tombé (that) I had fallen

8 donner → donné
to give   given

9 finir → fini
to finish   finished

0 vendre → vendu
to sell   sold

Compound Tenses: formation (ctd.)

Verbs taking the auxiliary avoir

Perfect tense: the present tense of **avoir** plus the past participle ($\rightarrow$**1**)

Pluperfect tense: the imperfect tense of **avoir** plus the past participle ($\rightarrow$**2**)

Future Perfect: the future tense of **avoir** plus the past participle ($\rightarrow$**3**)

Conditional Perfect: the conditional of **avoir** plus the past participle ($\rightarrow$**4**)

Past Anterior: the past historic of **avoir** plus the past participle ($\rightarrow$**5**)

Perfect Subjunctive: the present subjunctive of **avoir** plus the past participle ($\rightarrow$**6**)

Pluperfect Subjunctive: the imperfect subjunctive of **avoir** plus the past participle ($\rightarrow$**7**)

- For how to form the past participle of regular verbs see p. 22. The past participle of irregular verbs is given for each verb in the verb tables, pp. 74 ff.

- The past participle must agree in number and in gender with any preceding direct object (see p. 50)

Continued

1 PERFECT
j'ai donné | nous avons donné
tu as donné | vous avez donné
il/elle a donné | ils/elles ont donné

2 PLUPERFECT
j'avais donné | nous avions donné
tu avais donné | vous aviez donné
il/elle avait donné | ils/elles avaient donné

3 FUTURE PERFECT
j'aurai donné | nous aurons donné
tu auras donné | vous aurez donné
il/elle aura donné | ils/elles auront donné

4 CONDITIONAL PERFECT
j'aurais donné | nous aurions donné
tu aurais donné | vous auriez donné
il/elle aurait donné | ils/elles auraient donné

5 PAST ANTERIOR
j'eus donné | nous eûmes donné
tu eus donné | vous eûtes donné
il/elle eut donné | ils/elles eurent donné

6 PERFECT SUBJUNCTIVE
j'aie donné | nous ayons donné
tu aies donné | vous ayez donné
il/elle ait donné | ils/elles aient donné

7 PLUPERFECT SUBJUNCTIVE
j'eusse donné | nous eussions donné
tu eusses donné | vous eussiez donné
il/elle eût donné | ils/elles eussent donné

Compound Tenses: formation (ctd.)

Verbs taking the auxiliary être

Perfect tense:	the present tense of **être** plus the past participle (→**1**)
Pluperfect tense:	the imperfect tense of **être** plus the past participle (→**2**)
Future Perfect:	the future tense of **être** plus the past participle (→**3**)
Conditional Perfect:	the conditional of **être** plus the past participle (→**4**)
Past Anterior:	the past historic of **être** plus the past participle (→**5**)
Perfect Subjunctive:	the present subjunctive of **être** plus the past participle (→**6**)
Pluperfect Subjunctive:	the imperfect subjunctive of **être** plus the past participle (→**7**)

- For how to form the past participle of regular verbs see p. 22. The past participle of irregular verbs is given for each verb in the verb tables, pp. 74 ff.

- For agreement of past participles, see p. 50

- For a list of verbs and verb types that take the auxiliary **être**, see p. 28

Continued

1 PERFECT

je suis tombé(e)
tu es tombé(e)
il est tombé
elle est tombée

nous sommes tombé(e)s
vous êtes tombé(e)(s)
ils sont tombés
elles sont tombées

2 PLUPERFECT

j'étais tombé(e)
tu étais tombé(e)
il était tombé
elle était tombée

nous étions tombé(e)s
vous étiez tombé(e)(s)
ils étaient tombés
elles étaient tombées

3 FUTURE PERFECT

je serai tombé(e)
tu seras tombé(e)
il sera tombé
elle sera tombée

nous serons tombé(e)s
vous serez tombé(e)(s)
ils seront tombés
elles seront tombées

4 CONDITIONAL PERFECT

je serais tombé(e)
tu serais tombé(e)
il serait tombé
elle serait tombée

nous serions tombé(e)s
vous seriez tombé(e)(s)
ils seraient tombés
elles seraient tombées

5 PAST ANTERIOR

je fus tombé(e)
tu fus tombé(e)
il fut tombé
elle fut tombée

nous fûmes tombé(e)s
vous fûtes tombé(e)(s)
ils furent tombés
elles furent tombées

6 PERFECT SUBJUNCTIVE

je sois tombé(e)
tu sois tombé(e)
il soit tombé
elle soit tombée

nous soyons tombé(e)s
vous soyez tombé(e)(s)
ils soient tombés
elles soient tombées

7 PLUPERFECT SUBJUNCTIVE

je fusse tombé(e)
tu fusses tombé(e)
il fût tombé
elle fût tombée

nous fussions tombé(e)s
vous fussiez tombé(e)(s)
ils fussent tombés
elles fussent tombées

Compound Tenses (ctd.)

The following verbs take the auxiliary être

● Reflexive verbs (see p. 30) (→1)

● The following intransitive verbs (i.e. verbs which cannot take a direct object), largely expressing motion or a change of state:

aller	*to go* (→2)	**passer**	*to pass*
arriver	*to arrive; to happen*	**rentrer**	*to go back/in*
descendre	*to go/come down*	**rester**	*to stay* (→5)
devenir	*to become*	**retourner**	*to go back*
entrer	*to go/come in*	**revenir**	*to come back*
monter	*to go/come up*	**sortir**	*to go/come out*
mourir	*to die* (→3)	**tomber**	*to fall*
naître	*to be born*	**venir**	*to come* (→6)
partir	*to leave* (→4)		

● Of these, the following are conjugated with **avoir** when used transitively (i.e. with a direct object):

descendre	*to bring/take down*
entrer	*to bring/take in*
monter	*to bring/take up* (→7)
passer	*to pass; to spend* (→8)
rentrer	*to bring/take in*
retourner	*to turn over*
sortir	*to bring/take out* (→9)

● Note that the past participle must show an agreement in number and gender whenever the auxiliary is être EXCEPT FOR REFLEXIVE VERBS WHERE THE REFLEXIVE PRONOUN IS THE INDIRECT OBJECT (see p. 50)

1 je me suis couché(e)
I went to bed
tu t'es levé(e)
you got up

elle s'est trompée
she made a mistake
ils s'étaient battus
they had fought (one another)

2 elle est allée
she went

3 ils sont morts
they died

4 vous êtes partie
you left (*addressing a female person*)
vous êtes parties
you left (*addressing more than one female person*)

5 nous sommes resté(e)s
we stayed

6 elles étaient venues
they [female] had come

7 Il a monté les valises
He's taken up the cases

8 Nous avons passé trois semaines chez elle
We spent three weeks at her place

9 Avez-vous sorti la voiture?
Have you taken the car out?

Reflexive Verbs

A reflexive verb is one accompanied by a reflexive pronoun, e.g. **se lever** *to get up*; **se laver** *to wash (oneself)*. The pronouns are:

PERSON	SINGULAR	PLURAL
1st	**me (m')**	**nous**
2nd	**te (t')**	**vous**
3rd	**se (s')**	**se (s')**

The forms shown in brackets are used before a vowel, an **h** 'mute', or the pronoun **y** (→1)

- In positive commands, **te** changes to **toi** (→2)

- The reflexive pronoun 'reflects back' to the subject, but it is not always translated in English (→3)
  The plural pronouns are sometimes translated as *one another*, *each other* (the 'reciprocal' meaning) (→4)
  The reciprocal meaning may be emphasised by **l'un(e) l'autre (les un(e)s les autres)** (→5)

- Simple tenses of reflexive verbs are conjugated in exactly the same way as those of non-reflexive verbs except that the reflexive pronoun is always used. Compound tenses are formed with the auxiliary **être**. A sample reflexive verb is conjugated in full on pp. 34 and 35.

For agreement of past participles, see p. 32

Position of Reflexive Pronouns

- In constructions other than the imperative affirmative the pronoun comes before the verb (→6)
- In the imperative affirmative, the pronoun follows the verb and is attached to it by a hyphen (→7)

Continued

1 **Je m'ennuie**
I'm bored
Elle s'habille
She's dressing
Ils s'y intéressent
They are interested in it
2 **Assieds-toi**
Sit down
Tais-toi
Be quiet
3 **Je m'habille**
I'm dressing (myself)
Nous nous lavons
We're washing (ourselves)
Elle se lève
She gets up
4 **Nous nous aimons**
We like each other
Ils se ressemblent
They resemble one another
5 **Ils se regardent l'un l'autre**
They are looking at each other
6 **Je me couche tôt**
I go to bed early
Comment vous appelez-vous?
What is your name?
Il ne s'est pas réveillé
He hasn't woken up
Ne te lève pas
Don't get up
7 **Dépêche-toi**
Hurry (up)
Habillons-nous
Let's get dressed
Asseyez-vous
Sit down

32 VERBS

Reflexive Verbs (ctd.)

Past Participle Agreement

- In most reflexive verbs the reflexive pronoun is a DIRECT object pronoun (→1)

- When a direct object accompanies the reflexive verb the pronoun is then the INDIRECT object (→2)

- The past participle of a reflexive verb agrees in number and gender with a direct object which *precedes* the verb (usually, but not always, the reflexive pronoun) (→3)
  The past participle does not change if the direct object follows the verb (→4)

Here are some common reflexive verbs:

s'en aller	*to go away*	se hâter	*to hurry*
s'amuser	*to enjoy oneself*	se laver	*to wash (oneself)*
s'appeler	*to be called*	se lever	*to get up*
s'arrêter	*to stop*	se passer	*to happen*
s'asseoir	*to sit (down)*	se promener	*to go for a walk*
se baigner	*to go swimming*	se rappeler	*to remember*
se blesser	*to hurt oneself*	se ressembler	*to resemble each other*
se coucher	*to go to bed*	se retourner	*to turn round*
se demander	*to wonder*	se réveiller	*to wake up*
se dépêcher	*to hurry*	se sauver	*to run away*
se diriger	*to make one's way*	se souvenir de	*to remember*
s'endormir	*to fall asleep*	se taire	*to be quiet*
s'ennuyer	*to be/get bored*	se tromper	*to be mistaken*
se fâcher	*to get angry*	se trouver	*to be (situated)*
s'habiller	*to dress (oneself)*		

Continued

1 Je m'appelle
I'm called (*literally: I call myself*)
Asseyez-vous
Sit down (*literally: Seat yourself*)
Ils se lavent
They wash (themselves)

2 Elle se lave les mains
She's washing her hands (*literally: She's washing to herself the hands*)
Je me brosse les dents
I brush my teeth
Nous nous envoyons des cadeaux
We send presents to each other

3 'Je me suis endormi' a dit mon cousin
'I fell asleep' said my cousin
Pauline s'est dirigée vers la sortie
Pauline made her way towards the exit
Les deux frères se sont levés vers dix heures
The two brothers got up around ten o'clock
Elles se sont excusées de leur erreur
They apologised for their mistake
Est-ce que tu t'es blessée, Sophie?
Have you hurt yourself, Sophie?

4 Elle s'est lavé les cheveux
She (has) washed her hair
Nous nous sommes serré la main
We shook hands
Martine s'est cassé la jambe
Martine has broken her leg

Reflexive Verbs (ctd.)

Conjugation of: **se laver** to wash *(oneself)*

I SIMPLE TENSES

PRESENT

je me lave	nous nous lavons
tu te laves	vous vous lavez
il/elle se lave	ils/elles se lavent

IMPERFECT

je me lavais	nous nous lavions
tu te lavais	vous vous laviez
il/elle se lavait	ils/elles se lavaient

FUTURE

je me laverai	nous nous laverons
tu te laveras	vous vous laverez
il/elle se lavera	ils/elles se laveront

CONDITIONAL

je me laverais	nous nous laverions
tu te laverais	vous vous laveriez
il/elle se laverait	ils/elles se laveraient

PAST HISTORIC

je me lavai	nous nous lavâmes
tu te lavas	vous vous lavâtes
il/elle se lava	ils/elles se lavèrent

PRESENT SUBJUNCTIVE

je me lave	nous nous lavions
tu te laves	vous vous laviez
il/elle se lave	ils/elles se lavent

IMPERFECT SUBJUNCTIVE

je me lavasse	nous nous lavassions
tu te lavasses	vous vous lavassiez
il/elle se lavât	ils/elles se lavassent

Reflexive Verbs (ctd.)

Conjugation of: **se laver** *to wash (oneself)*

II COMPOUND TENSES

PERFECT

je me suis lavé(e)	nous nous sommes lavé(e)s
tu t'es lavé(e)	vous vous êtes lavé(e)(s)
il/elle s'est lavé(e)	ils/elles se sont lavé(e)s

PLUPERFECT

je m'étais lavé(e)	nous nous étions lavé(e)s
tu t'étais lavé(e)	vous vous étiez lavé(e)(s)
il/elle s'était lavé(e)	ils/elles s'étaient lavé(e)s

FUTURE PERFECT

je me serai lavé(e)	nous nous serons lavé(e)s
tu te seras lavé(e)	vous vous serez lavé(e)(s)
il/elle se sera lavé(e)	ils/elles se seront lavé(e)s

CONDITIONAL PERFECT

je me serais lavé(e)	nous nous serions lavé(e)s
tu te serais lavé(e)	vous vous seriez lavé(e)(s)
il/elle se serait lavé(e)	ils/elles se seraient lavé(e)s

PAST ANTERIOR

je me fus lavé(e)	nous nous fûmes lavé(e)s
tu te fus lavé(e)	vous vous fûtes lavé(e)(s)
il/elle se fut lavé(e)	ils/elles se furent lavé(e)s

PERFECT SUBJUNCTIVE

je me sois lavé(e)	nous nous soyons lavé(e)s
tu te sois lavé(e)	vous vous soyez lavé(e)(s)
il/elle se soit lavé(e)	ils/elles se soient lavé(e)s

PLUPERFECT SUBJUNCTIVE

je me fusse lavé(e)	nous nous fussions lavé(e)s
tu te fusses lavé(e)	vous vous fussiez lavé(e)(s)
il/elle se fût lavé(e)	ils/elles se fussent lavé(e)s

The Passive

In the passive, the subject *receives* the action (e.g. *I was hit*) as opposed to *performing* it (e.g. *I hit him*). In English the verb 'to be' is used with the past participle. In French the passive is formed in exactly the same way, i.e.:

a tense of **être** + past participle

The past participle agrees in number and gender with the subject (→1)

A sample verb is conjugated in the passive voice on pp. 38 and 39.

- The indirect object in French cannot become the subject in the passive:

    in **quelqu'un m'a donné un livre** the indirect object **m'** cannot become the subject of a passive verb (unlike English: *someone gave me a book→I was given a book*)

- The passive meaning is often expressed in French by:
    - **on** plus a verb in the active voice (→2)
    - a reflexive verb (see p. 30) (→3)

Continued

1 **Roger a été renvoyé**
  Roger has been dismissed
  Elle est très admirée
  She is greatly admired
  Ils le feront pourvu qu'ils soient payés
  They'll do it provided they're paid
  Les enfants seront punis
  The children will be punished
  J'aurais été insulté(e) si ...
  I would have been insulted if ...
  Les portes avaient été fermées
  The doors had been closed

2 **On leur a envoyé un cadeau**
  They were sent a present
  On nous a montré le jardin
  We were shown the garden
  On m'a dit que ...
  I was told that ...

3 **Ils se vendent 5 francs la pièce**
  They are sold for 5 francs each
  Ce mot ne s'emploie plus
  This word is no longer used

The Passive (ctd.)

Conjugation of: **être aimé** *to be liked*

PRESENT
je suis aimé(e)	nous sommes aimé(e)s
tu es aimé(e)	vous êtes aimé(e)(s)
il/elle est aimé(e)	ils/elles sont aimé(e)s

IMPERFECT
j'étais aimé(e)	nous étions aimé(e)s
tu étais aimé(e)	vous étiez aimé(e)(s)
il/elle était aimé(e)	ils/elles étaient aimé(e)s

FUTURE
je serai aimé(e)	nous serons aimé(e)s
tu seras aimé(e)	vous serez aimé(e)(s)
il/elle sera aimé(e)	ils/elles seront aimé(e)s

CONDITIONAL
je serais aimé(e)	nous serions aimé(e)s
tu serais aimé(e)	vous seriez aimé(e)(s)
il/elle serait aimé(e)	ils/elles seraient aimé(e)s

PAST HISTORIC
je fus aimé(e)	nous fûmes aimé(e)s
tu fus aimé(e)	vous fûtes aimé(e)(s)
il/elle fut aimé(e)	ils/elles furent aimé(e)s

PRESENT SUBJUNCTIVE
je sois aimé(e)	nous soyons aimé(e)s
tu sois aimé(e)	vous soyez aimé(e)(s)
il/elle soit aimé(e)	ils/elles soient aimé(e)s

IMPERFECT SUBJUNCTIVE
je fusse aimé(e)	nous fussions aimé(e)s
tu fusses aimé(e)	vous fussiez aimé(e)(s)
il/elle fût aimé(e)	ils/elles fussent aimé(e)s

The Passive (ctd.)

Conjugation of: **être aimé** *to be liked*

PERFECT
j'ai été aimé(e)
tu as été aimé(e)
il/elle a été aimé(e)

nous avons été aimé(e)s
vous avez été aimé(e)(s)
ils/elles ont été aimé(e)s

PLUPERFECT
j'avais été aimé(e)
tu avais été aimé(e)
il/elle avait été aimé(e)

nous avions été aimé(e)s
vous aviez été aimé(e)(s)
ils/elles avaient été aimé(e)s

FUTURE PERFECT
j'aurai été aimé(e)
tu auras été aimé(e)
il/elle aura été aimé(e)

nous aurons été aimé(e)s
vous aurez été aimé(e)(s)
ils/elles auront été aimé(e)s

CONDITIONAL PERFECT
j'aurais été aimé(e)
tu aurais été aimé(e)
il/elle aurait été aimé(e)

nous aurions été aimé(e)s
vous auriez été aimé(e)(s)
ils/elles auraient été aimé(e)s

PAST ANTERIOR
j'eus été aimé(e)
tu eus été aimé(e)
il/elle eut été aimé(e)

nous eûmes été aimé(e)s
vous eûtes été aimé(e)(s)
ils/elles eurent été aimé(e)s

PERFECT SUBJUNCTIVE
j'aie été aimé(e)
tu aies été aimé(e)
il/elle ait été aimé(e)

nous ayons été aimé(e)s
vous ayez été aimé(e)(s)
ils/elles aient été aimé(e)s

PLUPERFECT SUBJUNCTIVE
j'eusse été aimé(e)
tu eusses été aimé(e)
il/elle eût été aimé(e)

nous eussions été aimé(e)s
vous eussiez été aimé(e)(s)
ils/elles eussent été aimé(e)s

Impersonal Verbs

Impersonal verbs are used only in the infinitive and in the third person singular with the subject pronoun **il**, generally translated *it*.
e.g. **il pleut**
  it's raining
  il est facile de dire que ...
  it's easy to say that ...

The most common impersonal verbs are:

INFINITIVE	CONSTRUCTIONS
s'agir	**il s'agit de** + noun (→**1**)
	it's a question/matter of something,
	it's about something
	il s'agit de + infinitive (→**2**)
	it's a question/matter of doing; somebody must do
falloir	**il faut** + noun object (+ indirect object) (→**3**)
	(somebody) needs something, something is necessary (to somebody)
	il faut + infinitive (+ indirect object) (→**4**)
	it is necessary to do
	il faut que + subjunctive (→**5**)
	it is necessary to do, somebody must do
grêler	**il grêle**
	it's hailing
neiger	**il neige**
	it's snowing
pleuvoir	**il pleut** (→**6**)
	it's raining
tonner	**il tonne**
	it's thundering
valoir mieux	**il vaut mieux** + infinitive (→**7**)
	it's better to do
	il vaut mieux que + subjunctive (→**8**)
	it's better to do/that somebody does

Continued

1 Il ne s'agit pas d'argent
It isn't a question/matter of money
Il s'agit d'un nouvel élève
It's about a new pupil
De quoi s'agit-il?
What is it about?

2 Il s'agit de le prévenir
We must warn him

3 Il faut du courage pour faire ça
One needs courage to do that; Courage is needed to do that
Il me faut un verre de plus
I need an extra glass

4 Il faut partir
It is necessary to leave; We/I/You must leave★
Il me fallait partir
I had to leave

5 Il faut que vous partiez
You have to leave/You must leave
Il faudrait que je fasse mes valises
I should have to/ought to pack my cases

6 Il pleuvait à verse
It was raining heavily/It was pouring

7 Il vaut mieux refuser
It's better to refuse; You/He/I had better refuse★
Il vaudrait mieux rester
You/We/She had better stay★

8 Il vaudrait mieux que nous ne venions pas
It would be better if we didn't come; We'd better not come

★*The translation here obviously depends on context*

Impersonal Verbs (ctd.)

The following verbs are also commonly used in impersonal constructions:

INFINITIVE	CONSTRUCTIONS
avoir	**il y a** + noun (→1)
	there is/are
être	**il est** + noun (→2)
	it is; there are (very literary style)
	il est + adjective + **de** + infinitive (→3)
	it is
faire	**il fait** + adjective of weather (→4)
	it is
	il fait + noun depicting weather/dark/light etc.
	it is (→5)
manquer	**il manque** + noun (+ indirect object) (→6)
	there is/are ... missing, something is missing/lacking
paraître	**il paraît que** + subjunctive (→7)
	it seems/appears that
	il paraît + indirect object + **que** + indicative
	it seems/appears to somebody that (→8)
rester	**il reste** + noun (+ indirect object) (→9)
	there is/are ... left, (somebody) has something left
sembler	**il semble que** + subjunctive (→10)
	it seems/appears that
	il semble + indirect object + **que** + indicative
	it seems/appears to somebody that (→11)
suffire	**il suffit de** + infinitive (→12)
	it is enough to do
	il suffit de + noun (→13)
	something is enough, it only takes something

1 **Il y a du pain (qui reste)**
There is some bread (left)
Il n'y avait pas de lettres ce matin
There were no letters this morning

2 **Il est dix heures**
It's ten o'clock
Il est des gens qui ...
There are (some) people who ...

3 **Il était inutile de protester**
It was useless to protest
Il est facile de critiquer
Criticizing is easy

4 **Il fait beau/mauvais**
It's lovely/horrible weather

5 **Il faisait du soleil/du vent**
It was sunny/windy
Il fait jour/nuit
It's light/dark

6 **Il manque deux tasses**
There are two cups missing; Two cups are missing
Il manquait un bouton à la robe
The dress had a button missing

7 **Il paraît qu'ils partent demain**
It appears they are leaving tomorrow

8 **Il nous paraît certain qu'il aura du succès**
It seems certain to us that he'll be successful

9 **Il reste deux pains**
There are two loaves left
Il lui restait cinquante francs
He/She had fifty francs left

10 **Il semble que vous ayez raison**
It seems that you are right

11 **Il me semblait qu'il gagnait trop**
It seemed to me (that) he earned too much

12 **Il suffit de téléphoner pour réserver une place**
You need only phone to reserve a seat

13 **Il suffit d'une seule erreur pour tout gâcher**
One single error is enough to ruin everything

44 VERBS

The Infinitive

The infinitive is the form of the verb found in dictionary entries meaning 'to ...', e.g. **donner** *to give*, **vivre** *to live*.

There are three main types of verbal construction involving the infinitive:

- with no linking preposition (→**1**)
- with the linking preposition **à** (→**2**)
  (see also p. 64)
- with the linking preposition **de** (→**3**)
  (see also p. 64)

Verbs followed by an infinitive with no linking preposition

- **devoir, pouvoir, savoir, vouloir** and **falloir** (i.e. modal auxiliary verbs: p. 52) (→**1**)
- **valoir mieux**: see Impersonal Verbs, p. 40
- verbs of seeing or hearing e.g. **voir** *to see*, **entendre** *to hear* (→**4**)
- intransitive verbs of motion e.g. **aller** *to go*, **descendre** *to come/go down* (→**5**)
- **envoyer** *to send* (→**6**)
- **faillir** (→**7**)
- **faire** (→**8**)
- **laisser** *to let, allow* (→**9**)
- The following common verbs:

adorer	*to love*	
aimer	*to like, love*	(→**10**)
aimer mieux	*to prefer*	(→**11**)
compter	*to expect*	
désirer	*to wish, want*	(→**12**)
détester	*to hate*	(→**13**)
espérer	*to hope*	(→**14**)
oser	*to dare*	(→**15**)
préférer	*to prefer*	
sembler	*to seem*	(→**16**)
souhaiter	*to wish*	

Continued

1 Voulez-vous attendre?
Would you like to wait?

2 J'apprends à nager
I'm learning to swim

3 Essayez de venir
Try to come

4 Il nous a vus arriver
He saw us arriving

On les entend chanter
You can hear them singing

5 Allez voir Martine
Go and see Martine

Descends leur demander
Go down and ask them

6 Je l'ai envoyé les voir
I sent him to see them

7 J'ai failli tomber
I almost fell

8 Ne me faites pas rire!
Don't make me laugh!

J'ai fait réparer ma valise
I've had my case repaired

9 Laissez-moi passer
Let me pass

10 Il aime nous accompagner
He likes to come with us

11 J'aimerais mieux le choisir moi-même
I'd rather choose it myself

12 Elle ne désire pas venir
She doesn't wish to come

13 Je déteste me lever le matin
I hate getting up in the morning

14 Espérez-vous aller en vacances?
Are you hoping to go on holiday?

15 Nous n'avons pas osé y retourner
We haven't dared go back

16 Vous semblez être inquiet
You seem to be worried

The Infinitive: Set Expressions

The following are set in French with the meaning shown:

aller chercher	*to go for, to go and get*	(→1)
envoyer chercher	*to send for*	(→2)
entendre dire que	*to hear it said that*	(→3)
entendre parler de	*to hear of/about*	(→4)
faire entrer	*to show in*	(→5)
faire sortir	*to let out*	(→6)
faire venir	*to send for*	(→7)
laisser tomber	*to drop*	(→8)
vouloir dire	*to mean*	(→9)

The Perfect Infinitive

- The perfect infinitive is formed using the auxiliary verb **avoir** or **être** as appropriate with the past participle of the verb (→10)

- The perfect infinitive is found:
  - following the preposition **après** *after* (→11)
  - following certain verbal constructions (→12)

1 **Va chercher tes gants**
   Go and get your gloves
   Il est allé chercher Paul
   He's gone to get Paul

2 **J'ai envoyé chercher un médecin**
   I've sent for a doctor

3 **J'ai entendu dire qu'il est malade**
   I've heard it said that he's ill

4 **Je n'ai plus entendu parler de lui**
   I didn't hear anything more (said) of him

5 **Fais entrer nos invités**
   Show our guests in

6 **J'ai fait sortir le chat**
   I've let the cat out

7 **Je vous ai fait venir parce que ...**
   I sent for you because ...

8 **Il a laissé tomber le vase**
   He dropped the vase

9 **Qu'est-ce que cela veut dire?**
   What does that mean?

10 **avoir fini**
   to have finished
   être allé   **s'être levé**
   to have gone   to have got up

11 **Après avoir acheté le cadeau, il est revenu**
   After buying/having bought the present, he came back
   Après être parties, elles ont fondu en larmes
   After leaving/having left, they burst into tears
   Après nous être levé(e)s, nous avons lu les journaux
   After getting up/having got up, we read the papers

12 **pardonner à qn d'avoir fait**
   to forgive sb for doing/having done
   remercier qn d'avoir fait
   to thank sb for doing/having done
   regretter d'avoir fait
   to be sorry for doing/having done

The Present Participle

Formation

- 1st conjugation
  Replace the **-er** of the infinitive by **-ant** (→**1**)

    – Verbs ending in **-cer**: **c** changes to **ç** (→**2**)
    – Verbs ending in **-ger**: **g** changes to **ge** (→**3**)

- 2nd conjugation
  Replace the **-ir** of the infinitive by **-issant** (→**4**)

- 3rd conjugation
  Replace the **-re** of the infinitive by **-ant** (→**5**)

- For irregular present participles, see irregular verbs, p. 74 ff.

Uses

The present participle has a more restricted use in French than in English.

- Used as a verbal form, the present participle is invariable. It is found:
    – on its own, where it corresponds to the English present participle (→**6**)
    – following the preposition **en** (→**7**)
    Note, in particular, the construction:
    verb + **en** + present participle
    which is often translated by an English phrasal verb, i.e. one followed by a preposition like *to run down*, *to bring up* (→**8**)

- Used as an adjective, the present participle agrees in number and gender with the noun or pronoun (→**9**)

- Note, in particular, the use of **ayant** and **étant** – the present participles of the auxiliary verbs **avoir** and **être** – with a past participle (→**10**)

1 **donner** → **donnant**
   to give   giving
2 **lancer** → **lançant**
   to throw   throwing
3 **manger** → **mangeant**
   to eat   eating
4 **finir** → **finissant**
   to finish   finishing
5 **vendre** → **vendant**
   to sell   selling
6 **Paul, habitant près de Paris, a ...**
   Paul, living near Paris, has ...
   Elle, pensant que je serais fâché, a dit '...'
   She, thinking that I would be angry, said '...'
   Ils m'ont suivi, criant à tue-tête
   They followed me, shouting at the top of their voices
7 **En attendant sa sœur, Paul s'est endormi**
   While waiting for his sister, Paul fell asleep
   Téléphone-nous en arrivant chez toi
   Telephone us when you get home
   En appuyant sur ce bouton, on peut ...
   By pressing this button, you can ...
   Il s'est blessé en essayant de sauver un chat
   He hurt himself trying to rescue a cat
8 **sortir en courant**
   to run out (*literally: to go out running*)
   avancer en boitant
   to limp along (*literally: to go forward limping*)
9 **le soleil couchant**   **une lumière éblouissante**
   the setting sun   a dazzling light
   ils sont choquants   **elles étaient étonnantes**
   they are shocking   they were surprising
10 **Ayant mangé plus tôt, il ...**
   Having eaten earlier, he ...
   Étant arrivée en retard, elle ...
   Having arrived late, she ...

Past Participle Agreement

Like adjectives, a past participle must sometimes agree in number and gender with a noun or pronoun. For the rules of agreement, see below.

Example: **donné**

	MASCULINE	FEMININE
SING.	donné	donnée
PLUR.	donnés	données

- When the masculine singular form already ends in **-s**, no further **s** is added in the masculine plural, e.g. **pris** *taken*

Rules of Agreement in Compound Tenses

- When the auxiliary verb is **avoir**
  The past participle remains in the masculine singular form, unless a direct object precedes the verb. The past participle then agrees in number and gender with the preceding direct object (→1)

- When the auxiliary verb is **être**
  The past participle of a non-reflexive verb agrees in number and gender with the subject (→2)
  The past participle of a reflexive verb agrees in number and gender with the reflexive pronoun, if the pronoun is a direct object (→3)
  No agreement is made if the reflexive pronoun is an indirect object (→4)

The Past Participle as an adjective

The past participle agrees in number and gender with the noun or pronoun (→5)

1 **Voici le livre que vous avez demandé**
Here's the book you asked for
Laquelle avaient-elles choisie?
Which one had they chosen?
Les fils Courtin? Je les ai rencontrés à Rome
The Courtin boys? I met them in Rome
Il a gardé toutes les lettres qu'elle a écrites
He has kept all the letters she wrote

2 **Est-ce que ton frère est allé à l'étranger?**
Did your brother go abroad?
Elle était restée veuve
She had remained a widow
Les autres sont partis sans moi
The others have left without me
Mes cousines sont revenues hier
My cousins came back yesterday

3 **Tu t'es couché tard, Georges?**
Were you late getting to bed, George?
Suzanne s'est lavée à la hâte
Suzanne washed hurriedly
'Lui et moi nous nous sommes cachés' a-t-elle dit
'He and I hid,' she said
Les vendeuses se sont mises en grève
Shop assistants have gone on strike
Vous vous êtes brouillés?
Have you fallen out with each other?
Les amies s'étaient entraidées
The friends had helped one another

4 **Elle s'est lavé les mains**
She washed her hands
Ils se sont ressemblé
They looked like each other

5 **à un moment donné**   **la porte ouverte**
at a given time   the open door
ils sont bien connus   **elles semblent fatiguées**
they are well-known   they seem tired

Modal Auxiliary Verbs

- In French, the modal auxiliary verbs are: **devoir**, **pouvoir**, **savoir**, **vouloir** and **falloir**.

- They are followed by a verb in the infinitive and have the following meanings:

devoir   *to have to, must* (→1)
           to be due to (→2)
           in the conditional/conditional perfect:
           should/should have, ought/ought to have (→3)

pouvoir   *to be able to, can* (→4)
           to be allowed to, can, may (→5)
           indicating possibility: *may/might/could* (→6)

savoir   *to know how to, can* (→7)

vouloir   *to want/wish to* (→8)
           to be willing to, will (→9)
           in polite phrases (→10)

falloir   *to be necessary*: see Impersonal Verbs, p. 40

1 Je dois leur rendre visite
   I must visit them
   Elle a dû partir
   She (has) had to leave
   Il a dû mentir
   He must have lied

2 Vous devez revenir demain
   You're due (to come) back tomorrow
   Je devais attraper le train de neuf heures
   I was (supposed) to catch the nine o'clock train

3 Je devrais le faire
   I ought to do it
   J'aurais dû m'excuser
   I ought to have apologised

4 Il ne peut pas lever le bras
   He can't raise his arm
   Pouvez-vous réparer cette montre?
   Can you mend this watch?

5 Puis-je les accompagner?
   May I go with them?

6 Il peut encore changer d'avis
   He may change his mind yet
   Cela pourrait être vrai
   It could/might be true

7 Savez-vous conduire?
   Can you drive?
   Je ne sais pas faire une omelette
   I don't know how to make an omelette

8 Elle veut rester encore une nuit
   She wants to stay another night

9 Ils ne voulaient pas le faire
   They wouldn't do it/They weren't willing to do it
   Ma voiture ne veut pas démarrer
   My car won't start

0 Voulez-vous boire quelque chose?
   Would you like something to drink?

Use of Tenses

The Present

- Unlike English, French does not distinguish between the simple present (e.g. *I smoke, he reads, we live*) and the continuous present (e.g. *I am smoking, he is reading, we are living*) ($\rightarrow$**1**)
- To emphasise continuity, the following constructions may be used:

  être en train de faire

  être à faire ⎫ *to be doing* ($\rightarrow$**2**)
- French uses the present tense where English uses the perfect in the following cases:
  - with certain prepositions of time – notably **depuis** *for/since* – when an action begun in the past is continued in the present ($\rightarrow$**3**)

    Note, however, that the perfect is used as in English when the verb is negative or the action has been completed ($\rightarrow$**4**)
  - in the construction **venir de faire** *to have just done* ($\rightarrow$**5**)

The Future

The future is generally used as in English, but note the following:
- Immediate future time is often expressed by means of the present tense of **aller** plus an infinitive ($\rightarrow$**6**)
- In time clauses expressing future action, French uses the future where English uses the present ($\rightarrow$**7**)

The Future Perfect

- Used as in English to mean *shall/will have done* ($\rightarrow$**8**)
- In time clauses expressing future action, where English uses the perfect tense ($\rightarrow$**9**)

Continued

1 Je fume   I smoke OR I am smoking
  Il lit   He reads OR He is reading
  Nous habitons   We live OR We are living

2 Il est en train de travailler
  He's (busy) working

3 Paul apprend à nager depuis six mois
  Paul's been learning to swim for six months (*and still is*)
  Je suis debout depuis sept heures
  I've been up since seven
  Il y a longtemps que vous attendez?
  Have you been waiting long?
  Voilà deux semaines que nous sommes ici
  That's two weeks we've been here (*now*)

4 Ils ne se sont pas vus depuis des mois
  They haven't seen each other for months
  Elle est revenue il y a un an
  She came back a year ago

5 Suzanne vient de partir
  Suzanne has just left

6 Tu vas tomber si tu ne fais pas attention
  You'll fall if you're not careful
  Il va manquer le train
  He's going to miss the train
  Ça va prendre une demi-heure
  It'll take half an hour

7 Quand il viendra vous serez en vacances
  When he comes you'll be on holiday
  Faites-nous savoir aussitôt qu'elle arrivera
  Let us know as soon as she arrives

8 J'aurai fini dans une heure
  I shall have finished in an hour

9 Quand tu auras lu le roman, rends-le-moi
  When you've read the novel, give it back to me
  Je partirai dès que j'aurai fini
  I'll leave as soon as I've finished

Use of Tenses (ctd.)

The Imperfect

- The imperfect describes:
  - an action (or state) in the past without definite limits in time (→1)
  - habitual action(s) in the past (often translated by means of *would* or *used to*) (→2)
- French uses the imperfect tense where English uses the pluperfect in the following cases:
  - with certain prepositions of time – notably **depuis** *for/since* – when an action begun in the remoter past was continued in the more recent past (→3)
    Note, however, that the pluperfect *is* used as in English, when the verb is negative or the action has been completed (→4)
  - in the construction **venir de faire** *to have just done* (→5)

The Perfect

- The perfect is used to recount a completed action or event in the past. Note that this corresponds to a perfect tense or a simple past tense in English (→6)

The Past Historic

- Only ever used in *written, literary* French, the past historic recounts a completed action in the past, corresponding to a simple past tense in English (→7)

The Past Anterior

This tense is used instead of the pluperfect when a verb in another part of the sentence is in the past historic. That is

- in time clauses, after conjunctions like: **quand, lorsque** *when* **dès que, aussitôt que** *as soon as,* **après que** *after* (→8)
- after **à peine** *hardly, scarcely* (→9)

The Subjunctive

- In spoken French, the present subjunctive generally replaces the imperfect subjunctive. See also pp. 58 ff.

1   **Elle regardait par la fenêtre**
    She was looking out of the window
    Il pleuvait quand je suis sorti de chez moi
    It was raining when I left the house
    Nos chambres donnaient sur la plage
    Our rooms overlooked the beach

2   **Dans sa jeunesse il se levait à l'aube**
    In his youth he got up at dawn
    Nous causions des heures entières
    We would talk for hours on end
    Elle te taquinait, n'est-ce pas?
    She used to tease you, didn't she?

3   **Nous habitions à Rome depuis deux ans**
    We had been living in Rome for two years (*and still were*)
    Il était malade depuis 1965
    He had been ill since 1965
    Il y avait assez longtemps qu'il le faisait
    He had been doing it for quite a long time

4   **Voilà un an que je ne l'avais pas vu**
    I hadn't seen him for a year
    Il y avait une heure qu'elle était arrivée
    She had arrived one hour before

5   **Je venais de les rencontrer**
    I had just met them

6   **Nous sommes allés au bord de la mer**
    We went/have been to the seaside
    Il a refusé de nous aider
    He (has) refused to help us
    La voiture ne s'est pas arrêtée
    The car didn't stop/hasn't stopped

7   **Le roi mourut en 1592**
    The king died in 1592

8   **Quand il eut fini, il se leva**
    When he had finished, he got up

9   **A peine eut-il parlé qu'on frappa à la porte**
    He had scarcely spoken when there was a knock at the door

The Subjunctive: when to use it

(For how to form the subjunctive see pp. 6 ff.)

● After certain conjunctions

quoique
bien que } *although* (→**1**)

pour que
afin que } *so that* (→**2**)

pourvu que   *provided that* (→**3**)
jusqu'à ce que   *until* (→**4**)
avant que (... ne)   *before* (→**5**)
à moins que (... ne)   *unless* (→**6**)
de peur que (... ne)
de crainte que (... ne) } *for fear that, lest* (→**7**)

Note that the **ne** following the conjunctions in examples **5** to **7** has no translation value. It is often omitted in spoken informal French.

● After the conjunctions

de sorte que
de façon que } *so that* (indicating a *purpose*) (→**8**)
de manière que

When these conjunctions introduce a *result* and not a *purpose*, the subjunctive is not used (→**9**)

● After impersonal constructions which express necessity, possibility etc

il faut que
il est nécessaire que } *it is necessary that* (→**10**)

il est possible que   *it is possible that* (→**11**)
il semble que   *it seems that* (→**12**)
il vaut mieux que   *it is better that* (→**13**)
c'est dommage que   *it's a pity that* (→**14**)

Continued

1 **Bien qu'il travaille dur, il gagne peu**
Although he works hard, he doesn't earn much

2 **Emballez-les afin qu'ils ne s'abîment pas**
Wrap them so that they won't get damaged

3 **Nous irons ensemble pourvu que Martine soit d'accord**
We'll go together provided Martine agrees

4 **Reste ici jusqu'à ce que nous revenions**
Stay here until we come back

5 **Je le ferai avant que tu ne partes**
I'll do it before you leave

6 **A moins que je ne me trompe, ce doit être Paul**
Unless I'm mistaken, that must be Paul

7 **Parlez bas de peur qu'on ne vous entende**
Speak softly lest anyone hears you

8 **Retournez-vous de sorte que je vous voie**
Turn round so that I can see you

9 **Il refuse de le faire de sorte que je dois le faire moi-même**
He refuses to do it so that I have to do it myself

10 **Il faut que je vous parle immédiatement**
I must speak to you right away/It is necessary that I speak ...

11 **Il est possible qu'ils aient raison**
They may be right/It's possible that they are right

12 **Il semble qu'elle ne soit pas venue**
It appears that she hasn't come

13 **Il vaut mieux que vous restiez chez vous**
It's better that you stay at home

14 **C'est dommage qu'elle ait perdu son petit chien**
It's a shame/a pity that she's lost her puppy

The Subjunctive: when to use it (ctd.)

- After verbs of:
  - 'wishing'
    vouloir que
    désirer que ⎱ *to wish that, want* (→1)
    souhaiter que

  - 'fearing'
    craindre que
    avoir peur que ⎰ *to be afraid that* (→2)
    Note that **ne** in the first example has no translation value.
    It is often omitted in spoken informal French.

  - 'ordering', 'forbidding', 'allowing'
    ordonner que *to order that* (→3)
    défendre que *to forbid that* (→4)
    permettre que *to allow that* (→5)

  - opinion, expressing uncertainty
    croire que ⎱ *to think that* (→6)
    penser que
    douter que *to doubt that* (→7)

  - emotion (e.g. regret, shame, pleasure)
    regretter que *to be sorry that* (→8)
    être content/surpris etc **que** (→9)
    to be pleased/surprised etc that

- After a superlative (→10)

- After certain adjectives expressing some sort of 'uniqueness'
    dernier ... qui/que *last ... who/that*
    premier ... qui/que *first ... who/that*
    meilleur ... qui/que *best ... who/that* ⎱ (→11)
    seul ⎱... **qui/que** *only ... who/that*
    unique⎰

Continued

1 Nous voulons qu'elle soit contente
We want her to be happy (*literally: We want that she is happy*)
Désirez-vous que je le fasse?
Do you want me to do it?

2 Il craint que je ne le quitte
He's afraid that I'll leave him
Avez-vous peur qu'il ne revienne pas?
Are you afraid that he won't come back?

3 Il a ordonné qu'ils soient punis
He has ordered that they be punished

4 Elle défend que vous l'accompagniez
She forbids you to go with her

5 Permettez que nous vous aidions
Allow us to help you

6 Je ne pense pas qu'ils soient venus
I don't think they came

7 Nous doutons qu'il ait dit la vérité
We doubt that he told the truth

8 Je regrette que vous ne puissiez pas venir
I'm sorry that you cannot come

9 Je suis content que vous les aimiez
I'm pleased that you like them

10 la femme la plus aimable que je connaisse
the nicest woman I know
l'article le moins cher que j'aie acheté
the cheapest item I bought

11 Voici la dernière lettre qu'elle m'ait écrite
This is the last letter she wrote to me
Louis est la seule personne qui puisse me conseiller
Louis is the only person who can advise me

The Subjunctive: when to use it (ctd.)

- After   **si (...) que**   *however (...)*   (→**1**)
            qui que   *whoever*   (→**2**)
            quoi que   *whatever*   (→**3**)

- After **que** in the following:
  - to form the 3rd person imperative or to express a wish (→**4**)
  - when **que** has the meaning *if*, replacing **si** in a clause (→**5**)
  - when **que** has the meaning *whether* (→**6**)

- In relative clauses following certain types of indefinite and negative construction (→**7/8**)

- In set expressions (→**9**)

1 **si courageux que tu sois**
however brave you may be
si peu que ce soit
however little it is

2 **Qui que vous soyez, allez-vous-en!**
Whoever you are, go away!

3 **Quoi que nous fassions, ...**
Whatever we do, ...

4 **Qu'il entre!**
Let him come in!
Que cela vous serve de leçon!
Let that be a lesson to you!

5 **S'il fait beau et que tu te sentes mieux, nous irons ...**
If it's nice and you're feeling better, we'll go ...

6 **Que tu viennes ou non, je ...**
Whether you come or not, I ...

7 **Il cherche une maison qui ait deux caves**
He's looking for a house which has two cellars
(*subjunctive used since such a house may or may not exist*)
J'ai besoin d'un livre qui décrive l'art du mime
I need a book which describes the art of mime
(*subjunctive used since such a book may or may not exist*)

8 **Je n'ai rencontré personne qui la connaisse**
I haven't met anyone who knows her
Il n'y a rien qui puisse vous empêcher de ...
There's nothing that can prevent you from ...

9 **Vive le roi!**
Long live the king!
A Dieu ne plaise!
God forbid!

Verbs governing à and de

The following lists (p. 64 to 72) contain common verbal constructions using the prepositions **à** and **de**

Note the following abbreviations:

infin.	infinitive
perf. infin.	perfect infinitive*
qch	quelque chose
qn	quelqu'un
sb	somebody
sth	something

*For formation see p. 46

accuser qn de qch/de + perf. infin.	to accuse sb of sth/of doing, having done (**→1**)
accoutumer qn à qch/à + infin.	to accustom sb to sth/to doing
acheter qch à qn	to buy sth from sb/for sb (**→2**)
achever de + infin.	to end up doing
aider qn à + infin.	to help sb to do (**→3**)
s'amuser à + infin.	to have fun doing
s'apercevoir de qch	to notice sth (**→4**)
apprendre qch à qn	to teach sb sth
apprendre à + infin.	to learn to do (**→5**)
apprendre à qn à + infin.	to teach sb to do (**→6**)
s'approcher de qn/qch	to approach sb/sth (**→7**)
arracher qch à qn	to snatch sth from sb (**→8**)
(s')arrêter de + infin.	to stop doing (**→9**)
arriver à + infin.	to manage to do (**→10**)
assister à qch	to attend sth, be at sth
s'attendre à + infin.	to expect to do (**→11**)
blâmer qn de qch/de + perf. infin.	to blame sb for sth/for having done (**→12**)
cacher qch à qn	to hide sth from sb (**→13**)
cesser de + infin.	to stop doing (**→14**)

Continued

1 **Il m'a accusé d'avoir menti**
He accused me of lying

2 **Paul leur a acheté deux billets**
Paul bought two tickets from/for them

3 **Aidez-moi à porter ces valises**
Help me to carry these cases

4 **Il ne s'est pas aperçu de son erreur**
He didn't notice his mistake

5 **Elle apprend à lire**
She's learning to read

6 **Je lui apprends à nager**
I'm teaching him/her to swim

7 **Elle s'est approchée de moi, en disant '...'**
She came up to me, saying '...'

8 **Le voleur lui a arraché l'argent**
The thief snatched the money from him/her

9 **Arrêtez de parler!**
Stop talking!

10 **Je n'arrive pas à le comprendre**
I can't understand it

11 **Est-ce qu'elle s'attendait à le voir?**
Was she expecting to see him?

12 **Je ne la blâme pas de l'avoir fait**
I don't blame her for doing it

13 **Cache-les-leur!**
Hide them from them!

14 **Est-ce qu'il a cessé de pleuvoir?**
Has it stopped raining?

Verbs governing à and de (ctd.)

changer de qch	to change sth (→1)
se charger de qch/de + infin.	to see to sth/undertake to do
chercher à + infin.	to try to do
commander à qn de + infin.	to order sb to do (→2)
commencer à/de + infin.	to begin to do (→3)
conseiller à qn de + infin.	to advise sb to do (→4)
consentir à qch/à + infin.	to agree to sth/to do (→5)
continuer à/de + infin.	to continue to do
craindre de + infin.	to be afraid to do/of doing
décider de + infin.	to decide to do (→6)
se décider à + infin.	to make up one's mind to do
défendre à qn de + infin.	to forbid sb to do (→7)
demander qch à qn	to ask sb sth/for sth (→8)
demander à qn de + infin.	to ask sb to do (→9)
se dépêcher de + infin.	to hurry to do
dépendre de qn/qch	to depend on sb/sth
déplaire à qn	to displease sb (→10)
désobéir à qn	to disobey sb (→11)
dire à qn de + infin.	to tell sb to do (→12)
dissuader qn de + infin.	to dissuade sb from doing
douter de qch	to doubt sth
se douter de qch	to suspect sth
s'efforcer de + infin.	to strive to do
empêcher qn de + infin.	to prevent sb from doing (→13)
emprunter qch à qn	to borrow sth from sb (→14)
encourager qn à + infin.	to encourage sb to do (→15)
enlever qch à qn	to take sth away from sb
enseigner qch à qn	to teach sb sth
enseigner à qn à + infin.	to teach sb to do
entreprendre de + infin.	to undertake to do
essayer de + infin.	to try to do (→16)
éviter de + infin.	to avoid doing (→17)

Continued

1 **J'ai changé d'avis/de robe**
   I changed my mind/my dress
   Il faut changer de train à Bordeaux
   You have to change trains at Bordeaux

2 **Il leur a commandé de tirer**
   He ordered them to shoot

3 **Il commence à neiger**
   It's starting to snow

4 **Il leur a conseillé d'attendre**
   He advised them to wait

5 **Je n'ai pas consenti à l'aider**
   I haven't agreed to help him/her

6 **Qu'est-ce que vous avez décidé de faire?**
   What have you decided to do?

7 **Je leur ai défendu de sortir**
   I've forbidden them to go out

8 **Je lui ai demandé l'heure**
   I asked him/her the time
   Il lui a demandé un livre
   He asked him/her for a book

9 **Demande à Gabrielle de le faire**
   Ask Gabrielle to do it

10 **Leur attitude lui déplaît**
   He/She doesn't like their attitude

11 **Ils lui désobéissent souvent**
   They often disobey him/her

12 **Dites-leur de se taire**
   Tell them to be quiet

13 **Le bruit m'empêche de travailler**
   The noise is preventing me from working

14 **Puis-je vous emprunter ce stylo?**
   May I borrow this pen from you?

15 **Elle encourage ses enfants à être indépendants**
   She encourages her children to be independent

16 **Essayez d'arriver avant les autres**
   Try to arrive before the others

17 **Pourquoi avez-vous évité de répondre?**
   Why did you avoid answering?

Verbs governing à and de (ctd.)

s'excuser de qch/de + (perf.) infin.	to apologise for sth/for doing, having done (→1)
exceller à + infin.	to excel at doing
se fâcher de qch	to be annoyed at sth
feindre de + infin.	to pretend to do (→2)
féliciter qn de qch/de + (perf.) infin.	to congratulate sb on sth/on doing, having done (→3)
se fier à qn	to trust sb (→4)
finir de + infin.	to finish doing (→5)
forcer qn à + infin.	to force sb to do
habituer qn à + infin.	to accustom sb to doing
s'habituer à + infin.	to get/be used to doing (→6)
se hâter de + infin.	to hurry to do
hésiter à + infin.	to hesitate to do
interdire à qn de + infin.	to forbid sb to do (→7)
s'intéresser à qn/qch/à + infin.	to be interested in sb/sth/in doing (→8)
inviter qn à + infin.	to invite sb to do (→9)
jouer à (+ sports, games)	to play (→10)
jouer de (+ musical instruments)	to play (→11)
jouir de qch	to enjoy sth (→12)
jurer de + infin.	to swear to do
louer qn de qch	to praise sb for sth
manquer à qn	to be missed by sb (→13)
manquer de qch	to lack sth
manquer de + infin.	to fail to do (→14)
se marier à qn	to marry sb
se méfier de qn	to distrust sb
menacer de + infin.	to threaten to do (→15)
mériter de + infin.	to deserve to do (→16)
se mettre à + infin.	to begin to do
se moquer de qn/qch	to make fun of sb/sth
négliger de + infin.	to fail to do

Continued

1 **Je m'excuse d'être (arrivé) en retard**
  I apologise for being (arriving) late

2 **Elle feint de dormir**
  She's pretending to be asleep

3 **Je l'ai félicitée d'avoir gagné**
  I congratulated her on winning

4 **Je ne me fie pas à elle**
  I don't trust her

5 **Avez-vous fini de lire ce journal?**
  Have you finished reading this newspaper?

6 **Est-ce que vous vous habituez à vous lever tôt?**
  Are you getting used to getting up early?

7 **Il a interdit aux enfants de jouer avec eux**
  He's forbidden the children to play with them

8 **Elle s'intéresse beaucoup aux sports**
  She's very interested in sport

9 **Il m'a invitée à danser**
  He asked me to dance

10 **Elle joue au tennis et au hockey**
  She plays tennis and hockey

11 **Il joue du piano et de la guitare**
  He plays the piano and the guitar

12 **Il jouit d'une santé solide**
  He enjoys good health

13 **Tu manques à tes parents**
  Your parents miss you

14 **Ne manquez pas de l'envoyer**
  Don't forget to send it/Be sure to send it

15 **Elle a menacé de se tuer**
  She threatened to kill herself

16 **Ils méritent d'être punis**
  They deserve to be punished

Verbs governing à and de (ctd.)

nuire à qch	to harm sth (→1)
obéir à qn	to obey sb (→2)
obliger qn à + infin.	to oblige sb to do
s'occuper de qch/qn	to look after sth/sb (→3)
offrir de + infin.	to offer to do (→4)
omettre de + infin.	to fail to do
ordonner à qn de + infin.	to order sb to do (→5)
ôter qch à qn	to take sth away from sb
oublier de + infin.	to forget to do
pardonner qch à qn	to forgive sb for sth
pardonner à qn de + perf. infin.	to forgive sb for having done (→6)
parvenir à + infin.	to manage to do
se passer de qch	to do/go without sth (→7)
penser à qn/qch	to think about sb/sth (→8)
permettre qch à qn	to allow sb sth
permettre à qn de + infin.	to allow sb to do (→9)
persister à + infin.	to persist in doing
persuader qn de + infin.	to persuade sb to do (→10)
se plaindre de qch	to complain about sth
plaire à qn	to please sb (→11)
pousser qn à + infin.	to urge sb to do
prendre qch à qn	to take sth from sb (→12)
préparer qn à + infin.	to prepare sb to do
se préparer à + infin.	to get ready to do
prier qn de + infin.	to beg sb to do
profiter de qch/de + infin.	to take advantage of sth/of doing
promettre à qn de + infin.	to promise sb to do (→13)
proposer de + infin.	to suggest doing (→14)
punir qn de qch	to punish sb for sth (→15)
récompenser qn de qch	to reward sb for sth
réfléchir à qch	to think about sth
refuser de + infin.	to refuse to do (→16)

Continued

1 **Ce mode de vie va nuire à sa santé**
   This lifestyle will damage her health

2 **Ils obéissent toujours à leur père**
   They always obey their father

3 **Je m'occupe de ma nièce**
   I'm looking after my niece

4 **Simon a offert de nous accompagner**
   Simon has offered to go with us

5 **Les soldats leur ont ordonné de se rendre**
   The soldiers ordered them to give themselves up

6 **Est-ce que tu as pardonné à Claude de l'avoir dit?**
   Have you forgiven Claude for saying it?

7 **Nous nous sommes passés de nourriture pendant plusieurs
   jours**
   We went without food for several days

8 **Je pense souvent à toi**
   I often think about you

9 **Permettez-moi de continuer, s'il vous plaît**
   Allow me to go on, please

10 **Elle nous a persuadés de rester**
   She persuaded us to stay

11 **Est-ce que ce genre de film lui plaît?**
   Does he/she like this kind of film?

12 **Je lui ai pris son revolver**
   I took his gun from him

13 **Ils ont promis à Marie de venir**
   They promised Marie that they would come

14 **J'ai proposé de les inviter**
   I suggested inviting them

15 **Il a été puni de sa malhonnêteté**
   He has been punished for his dishonesty

16 **Il a refusé de coopérer**
   He has refused to cooperate

Verbs governing à and de (ctd.)

regretter de + perf. infin.	to regret doing, having done (→**1**)
remercier qn de qch/de + perf. infin.	to thank sb for sth/for doing, having done (→**2**)
renoncer à qch/à + infin.	to give sth up/give up doing
reprocher qch à qn	to reproach sb with sth (→**3**)
résister à qch	to resist sth (→**4**)
résoudre de + infin.	to resolve to do
ressembler à qn/qch	to look/be like sb/sth (→**5**)
réussir à + infin.	to manage to do (→**6**)
rire de qn/qch	to laugh at sb/sth
risquer de + infin.	to risk doing (→**7**)
servir à qch/à + infin.	to be used for sth/for doing (→**8**)
se servir de qch	to use sth; to help oneself to sth (→**9**)
songer à + infin.	to think of doing
se souvenir de qn/qch/de + perf. infin.	to remember sb/sth/doing, having done (→**10**)
succéder à qn	to succeed sb
survivre à qn	to outlive sb (→**11**)
tâcher de + infin.	to try to do
tarder à + infin.	to delay doing (→**12**)
tendre à + infin.	to tend to do
tenir à + infin.	to be keen to do (→**13**)
tenter de + infin.	to try to do (→**15**)
se tromper de qch	to be wrong about sth (→**16**)
venir de* + infin.	to have just done (→**17**)
vivre de qch	to live on sth
voler qch à qn	to steal sth from sb

*See also Use of Tenses, pp. 54 and 56

1 Je regrette de ne pas vous avoir écrit
I'm sorry for not writing to you

2 Nous les avons remerciés de leur gentillesse
We thanked them for their kindness

3 On lui reproche sa lâcheté
They're reproaching him with cowardice/being a coward

4 Comment résistez-vous à la tentation?
How do you resist temptation?

5 Elles ressemblent beaucoup à leur mère
They look very like their mother

6 Vous avez réussi à me convaincre
You've managed to convince me

7 Vous risquez de tomber en faisant cela
You risk falling doing that

8 Ce bouton sert à régler le volume
This knob is (used) for adjusting the volume

9 Il s'est servi d'un tournevis pour l'ouvrir
He used a screwdriver to open it

10 Vous vous souvenez de Gabrielle?
Do you remember Gabrielle?
Il ne se souvient pas de l'avoir perdu
He doesn't remember losing it

11 Elle a survécu à son mari
She outlived her husband

12 Tâchez de ne pas être en retard!
Try not to be late!

13 Il n'a pas tardé à prendre une décision
He was not long in taking a decision

14 Elle tient à le faire elle-même
She's keen to do it herself

15 J'ai tenté de la comprendre
I've tried to understand her

16 Je me suis trompé de route
I took the wrong road

17 Mon père vient de téléphoner   **Nous venions de nous lever**
My father's just phoned   We had just got up

Irregular Verbs

The verbs listed opposite and conjugated on pp. 76 to 131 provide the main patterns for irregular verbs. The verbs are grouped opposite according to their infinitive ending (except **avoir** and **être**), and are shown in the following tables in alphabetical order.

In the tables, the most important irregular verbs are given in their most common simple tenses, together with the imperative and the present participle.

The auxiliary (**avoir** or **être**) is also shown for each verb, together with the past participle, to enable you to form all the compound tenses, as on pp. 24 and 26.

- For a fuller list of irregular verbs, the reader is referred to Collins Gem French Verb Tables, which shows you how to conjugate some 2000 French verbs.

Continued

	avoir		
	être		
'-er':	aller	'-re':	battre
	envoyer		boire
			connaître
'-ir':	acquérir		coudre
	bouillir		craindre
	courir		croire
	cueillir		croître
	dormir		cuire
	fuir		dire
	haïr		écrire
	mourir		faire
	ouvrir		lire
	partir		mettre
	sentir		moudre
	servir		naître
	sortir		paraître
	tenir		plaire
	venir		prendre
	vêtir		résoudre
			rire
'-oir':	s'asseoir		rompre
	devoir		suffire
	falloir		suivre
	pleuvoir		se taire
	pouvoir		vaincre
	recevoir		vivre
	savoir		
	valoir		
	voir		
	vouloir		

acquérir *to acquire*   Auxiliary: **avoir**

PAST PARTICIPLE
acquis

PRESENT PARTICIPLE
acquérant

IMPERATIVE
acquiers
acquérons
acquérez

PRESENT
    j'**acquiers**
  tu **acquiers**
    il **acquiert**
nous **acquérons**
vous **acquérez**
  ils **acquièrent**

IMPERFECT
    j'**acquérais**
  tu **acquérais**
    il **acquérait**
nous **acquérions**
vous **acquériez**
  ils **acquéraient**

FUTURE
    j'**acquerrai**
  tu **acquerras**
    il **acquerra**
nous **acquerrons**
vous **acquerrez**
  ils **acquerront**

CONDITIONAL
    j'**acquerrais**
  tu **acquerrais**
    il **acquerrait**
nous **acquerrions**
vous **acquerriez**
  ils **acquerraient**

PRESENT SUBJUNCTIVE
    j'**acquière**
  tu **acquières**
    il **acquière**
nous **acquérions**
vous **acquériez**
  ils **acquièrent**

PAST HISTORIC
    j'**acquis**
  tu **acquis**
    il **acquit**
nous **acquîmes**
vous **acquîtes**
  ils **acquirent**

aller *to go*   Auxiliary: **être**

PAST PARTICIPLE	IMPERATIVE
allé	**va**
	allons
PRESENT PARTICIPLE	allez
allant	

PRESENT	IMPERFECT
je **vais**	j'allais
tu **vas**	tu allais
il **va**	il allait
nous allons	nous allions
vous allez	vous alliez
ils **vont**	ils allaient

FUTURE	CONDITIONAL
j'**irai**	j'**irais**
tu **iras**	tu **irais**
il **ira**	il **irait**
nous **irons**	nous **irions**
vous **irez**	vous **iriez**
ils **iront**	ils **iraient**

PRESENT SUBJUNCTIVE	PAST HISTORIC
j'**aille**	j'allai
tu **ailles**	tu allas
il **aille**	il alla
nous allions	nous allâmes
vous alliez	vous allâtes
ils **aillent**	ils allèrent

s'asseoir *to sit down*   Auxiliary: **être**

PAST PARTICIPLE
assis

PRESENT PARTICIPLE
s'asseyant

IMPERATIVE
assieds-toi
asseyons-nous
asseyez-vous

PRESENT	IMPERFECT
je m'assieds	je m'asseyais
tu t'assieds	tu t'asseyais
il s'assied	il s'asseyait
nous nous asseyons	nous nous asseyions
vous vous asseyez	vous vous asseyiez
ils s'asseyent	ils s'asseyaient

FUTURE	CONDITIONAL
je m'assiérai	je m'assiérais
tu t'assiéras	tu t'assiérais
il s'assiéra	il s'assiérait
nous nous assiérons	nous nous assiérions
vous vous assiérez	vous vous assiériez
ils s'assiéront	ils s'assiéraient

PRESENT SUBJUNCTIVE	PAST HISTORIC
je m'asseye	je m'assis
tu t'asseyes	tu t'assis
il s'asseye	il s'assit
nous nous asseyions	nous nous assîmes
vous vous asseyiez	vous vous assîtes
ils s'asseyent	ils s'assirent

avoir *to have* Auxiliary: **avoir**

PAST PARTICIPLE
  eu

PRESENT PARTICIPLE
  ayant

IMPERATIVE
  aie
  ayons
  ayez

PRESENT	IMPERFECT
j'ai	j'avais
tu as	tu avais
il a	il avait
nous avons	nous avions
vous avez	vous aviez
ils ont	ils avaient

FUTURE	CONDITIONAL
j'aurai	j'aurais
tu auras	tu aurais
il aura	il aurait
nous aurons	nous aurions
vous aurez	vous auriez
ils auront	ils auraient

PRESENT SUBJUNCTIVE	PAST HISTORIC
j'aie	j'eus
tu aies	tu eus
il ait	il eut
nous ayons	nous eûmes
vous ayez	vous eûtes
ils aient	ils eurent

battre *to beat*   Auxiliary: **avoir**

PAST PARTICIPLE	IMPERATIVE
battu	**bats**
	battons
PRESENT PARTICIPLE	battez
battant	

PRESENT	IMPERFECT
je bats	je battais
tu bats	tu battais
il bat	il battait
nous battons	nous battions
vous battez	vous battiez
ils battent	ils battaient

FUTURE	CONDITIONAL
je battrai	je battrais
tu battras	tu battrais
il battra	il battrait
nous battrons	nous battrions
vous battrez	vous battriez
ils battront	ils battraient

PRESENT SUBJUNCTIVE	PAST HISTORIC
je batte	je battis
tu battes	tu battis
il batte	il battit
nous battions	nous battîmes
vous battiez	vous battîtes
ils battent	ils battirent

boire *to drink*   Auxiliary: **avoir**

PAST PARTICIPLE
  bu

PRESENT PARTICIPLE
  buvant

IMPERATIVE
  bois
  buvons
  buvez

PRESENT	IMPERFECT
je bois	**je buvais**
tu bois	**tu buvais**
il boit	**il buvait**
nous buvons	**nous buvions**
vous buvez	**vous buviez**
ils boivent	**ils buvaient**

FUTURE	CONDITIONAL
je boirai	je boirais
tu boiras	tu boirais
il boira	il boirait
nous boirons	nous boirions
vous boirez	vous boiriez
ils boiront	ils boiraient

PRESENT SUBJUNCTIVE	PAST HISTORIC
je boive	je bus
tu boives	tu bus
il boive	il but
nous buvions	**nous bûmes**
vous buviez	**vous bûtes**
ils boivent	**ils burent**

bouillir *to boil*   Auxiliary: **avoir**

PAST PARTICIPLE	IMPERATIVE
bouilli	**bous**
	bouillons
PRESENT PARTICIPLE	**bouillez**
bouillant	

PRESENT	IMPERFECT
je bous	**je bouillais**
tu bous	**tu bouillais**
il bout	**il bouillait**
nous bouillons	**nous bouillions**
vous bouillez	**vous bouilliez**
ils bouillent	**ils bouillaient**

FUTURE	CONDITIONAL
je bouillirai	je bouillirais
tu bouilliras	tu bouillirais
il bouillira	il bouillirait
nous bouillirons	nous bouillirions
vous bouillirez	vous bouilliriez
ils bouilliront	ils bouilliraient

PRESENT SUBJUNCTIVE	PAST HISTORIC
je bouille	je bouillis
tu bouilles	tu bouillis
il bouille	il bouillit
nous bouillions	nous bouillîmes
vous bouilliez	vous bouillîtes
ils bouillent	ils bouillirent

connaître *to know*   Auxiliary: **avoir**

PAST PARTICIPLE
connu

PRESENT PARTICIPLE
connaissant

IMPERATIVE
connais
connaissons
connaissez

PRESENT
je connais
tu connais
il connaît
nous connaissons
vous connaissez
ils connaissent

IMPERFECT
je connaissais
tu connaissais
il connaissait
nous connaissions
vous connaissiez
ils connaissaient

FUTURE
je connaîtrai
tu connaîtras
il connaîtra
nous connaîtrons
vous connaîtrez
ils connaîtront

CONDITIONAL
je connaîtrais
tu connaîtrais
il connaîtrait
nous connaîtrions
vous connaîtriez
ils connaîtraient

PRESENT SUBJUNCTIVE
je connaisse
tu connaisses
il connaisse
nous connaissions
vous connaissiez
ils connaissent

PAST HISTORIC
je connus
tu connus
il connut
nous connûmes
vous connûtes
ils connurent

coudre to sew   Auxiliary: **avoir**

PAST PARTICIPLE
cousu

PRESENT PARTICIPLE
cousant

IMPERATIVE
couds
cousons
cousez

PRESENT	IMPERFECT
je couds	je cousais
tu couds	tu cousais
il coud	il cousait
nous cousons	**nous cousions**
vous cousez	**vous cousiez**
ils cousent	**ils cousaient**

FUTURE	CONDITIONAL
je coudrai	je coudrais
tu coudras	tu coudrais
il coudra	il coudrait
nous coudrons	nous coudrions
vous coudrez	vous coudriez
ils coudront	ils coudraient

PRESENT SUBJUNCTIVE	PAST HISTORIC
je couse	**je cousis**
tu couses	**tu cousis**
il couse	**il cousit**
nous cousions	**nous cousîmes**
vous cousiez	**vous cousîtes**
ils cousent	**ils cousirent**

courir *to run*   Auxiliary: **avoir**

PAST PARTICIPLE
 couru

IMPERATIVE
 cours
 courons
 courez

PRESENT PARTICIPLE
 courant

PRESENT	IMPERFECT
je **cours**	je **courais**
tu **cours**	tu **courais**
il **court**	il **courait**
nous **courons**	nous **courions**
vous **courez**	vous **couriez**
ils **courent**	ils **couraient**

FUTURE	CONDITIONAL
je **courrai**	je **courrais**
tu **courras**	tu **courrais**
il **courra**	il **courrait**
nous **courrons**	nous **courrions**
vous **courrez**	vous **courriez**
ils **courront**	ils **courraient**

PRESENT SUBJUNCTIVE	PAST HISTORIC
je **coure**	je **courus**
tu **coures**	tu **courus**
il **coure**	il **courut**
nous **courions**	nous **courûmes**
vous **couriez**	vous **courûtes**
ils **courent**	ils **coururent**

craindre *to fear*

Auxiliary: **avoir**

PAST PARTICIPLE
craint

PRESENT PARTICIPLE
craignant

IMPERATIVE
crains
craignons
craignez

PRESENT	IMPERFECT
je **crains**	je **craignais**
tu **crains**	tu **craignais**
il **craint**	il **craignait**
nous **craignons**	nous **craignions**
vous **craignez**	vous **craigniez**
ils **craignent**	ils **craignaient**

FUTURE	CONDITIONAL
je **craindrai**	je **craindrais**
tu **craindras**	tu **craindrais**
il **craindra**	il **craindrait**
nous **craindrons**	nous **craindrions**
vous **craindrez**	vous **craindriez**
ils **craindront**	ils **craindraient**

PRESENT SUBJUNCTIVE	PAST HISTORIC
je **craigne**	je **craignis**
tu **craignes**	tu **craignis**
il **craigne**	il **craignit**
nous **craignions**	nous **craignîmes**
vous **craigniez**	vous **craignîtes**
ils **craignent**	ils **craignirent**

Verbs ending in **-eindre** and **-oindre** are conjugated similarly

croire *to believe*   Auxiliary: **avoir**

PAST PARTICIPLE
cru

PRESENT PARTICIPLE
croyant

IMPERATIVE
crois
croyons
croyez

PRESENT	IMPERFECT
je crois	**je croyais**
tu crois	**tu croyais**
il croit	il croyait
nous croyons	nous croyions
vous croyez	vous croyiez
ils croient	**ils croyaient**

FUTURE	CONDITIONAL
je croirai	je croirais
tu croiras	tu croirais
il croira	il croirait
nous croirons	nous croirions
vous croirez	vous croiriez
ils croiront	ils croiraient

PRESENT SUBJUNCTIVE	PAST HISTORIC
je croie	**je crus**
tu croies	**tu crus**
il croie	**il crut**
nous croyions	**nous crûmes**
vous croyiez	**vous crûtes**
ils croient	**ils crurent**

croître *to grow*   Auxiliary: **avoir**

PAST PARTICIPLE
crû

PRESENT PARTICIPLE
croissant

IMPERATIVE
croîs
croissons
croissez

PRESENT	IMPERFECT
je **croîs**	je **croissais**
tu **croîs**	tu **croissais**
il **croît**	il **croissait**
nous **croissons**	nous **croissions**
vous **croissez**	vous **croissiez**
ils **croissent**	ils **croissaient**

FUTURE	CONDITIONAL
je croîtrai	je croîtrais
tu croîtras	tu croîtrais
il croîtra	il croîtrait
nous croîtrons	nous croîtrions
vous croîtrez	vous croîtriez
ils croîtront	ils croîtraient

PRESENT SUBJUNCTIVE	PAST HISTORIC
je **croisse**	je **crûs**
tu **croisses**	tu **crûs**
il **croisse**	il **crût**
nous **croissions**	nous **crûmes**
vous **croissiez**	vous **crûtes**
ils **croissent**	ils **crûrent**

cueillir *to pick*   Auxiliary: **avoir**

PAST PARTICIPLE
cueilli

IMPERATIVE
cueille
cueillons
cueillez

PRESENT PARTICIPLE
cueillant

PRESENT
je **cueille**
tu **cueilles**
il **cueille**
nous **cueillons**
vous **cueillez**
ils **cueillent**

IMPERFECT
je **cueillais**
tu **cueillais**
il **cueillait**
nous **cueillions**
vous **cueilliez**
ils **cueillaient**

FUTURE
je **cueillerai**
tu **cueilleras**
il **cueillera**
nous **cueillerons**
vous **cueillerez**
ils **cueilleront**

CONDITIONAL
je **cueillerais**
tu **cueillerais**
il **cueillerait**
nous **cueillerions**
vous **cueilleriez**
ils **cueilleraient**

PRESENT SUBJUNCTIVE
je **cueille**
tu **cueilles**
il **cueille**
nous **cueillions**
vous **cueilliez**
ils **cueillent**

PAST HISTORIC
je **cueillis**
tu **cueillis**
il **cueillit**
nous **cueillîmes**
vous **cueillîtes**
ils **cueillirent**

cuire *to cook*	Auxiliary: **avoir**

PAST PARTICIPLE	IMPERATIVE
cuit	cuis
	cuisons
PRESENT PARTICIPLE	**cuisez**
cuisant	

PRESENT	IMPERFECT
je cuis	**je cuisais**
tu cuis	**tu cuisais**
il cuit	**il cuisait**
nous cuisons	**nous cuisions**
vous cuisez	**vous cuisiez**
ils cuisent	**ils cuisaient**

FUTURE	CONDITIONAL
je cuirai	je cuirais
tu cuiras	tu cuirais
il cuira	il cuirait
nous cuirons	nous cuirions
vous cuirez	vous cuiriez
ils cuiront	ils cuiraient

PRESENT SUBJUNCTIVE	PAST HISTORIC
je cuise	**je cuisis**
tu cuises	**tu cuisis**
il cuise	**il cuisit**
nous cuisions	**nous cuisîmes**
vous cuisiez	**vous cuisîtes**
ils cuisent	**ils cuisirent**

nuire *to harm*, conjugated similarly, but past participle **nui**

devoir *to have to; to owe*   Auxiliary: **avoir**

PAST PARTICIPLE
dû

IMPERATIVE
dois
devons
devez

PRESENT PARTICIPLE
devant

PRESENT	IMPERFECT
je **dois**	je **devais**
tu **dois**	tu **devais**
il **doit**	il **devait**
nous **devons**	nous **devions**
vous **devez**	vous **deviez**
ils **doivent**	ils **devaient**

FUTURE	CONDITIONAL
je **devrai**	je **devrais**
tu **devras**	tu **devrais**
il **devra**	il **devrait**
nous **devrons**	nous **devrions**
vous **devrez**	vous **devriez**
ils **devront**	ils **devraient**

PRESENT SUBJUNCTIVE	PAST HISTORIC
je **doive**	je **dus**
tu **doives**	tu **dus**
il **doive**	il **dut**
nous **devions**	nous **dûmes**
vous **deviez**	vous **dûtes**
ils **doivent**	ils **durent**

dire *to say, tell*   Auxiliary: **avoir**

PAST PARTICIPLE	IMPERATIVE
dit	dis
	disons
PRESENT PARTICIPLE	**dites**
disant	

PRESENT	IMPERFECT
je dis	**je disais**
tu dis	**tu disais**
il dit	**il disait**
nous disons	**nous disions**
vous dites	**vous disiez**
ils disent	**ils disaient**

FUTURE	CONDITIONAL
je dirai	je dirais
tu diras	tu dirais
il dira	il dirait
nous dirons	nous dirions
vous direz	vous diriez
ils diront	ils diraient

PRESENT SUBJUNCTIVE	PAST HISTORIC
je dise	**je dis**
tu dises	**tu dis**
il dise	**il dit**
nous disions	**nous dîmes**
vous disiez	**vous dîtes**
ils disent	**ils dirent**

---

interdire *to forbid*, conjugated similarly, but 2nd. person plural c the present tense is **vous interdisez**

dormir *to sleep*   Auxiliary: **avoir**

PAST PARTICIPLE
  dormi

IMPERATIVE
  dors
  dormons
  dormez

PRESENT PARTICIPLE
  dormant

PRESENT
  je **dors**
  tu **dors**
  il **dort**
  nous **dormons**
  vous **dormez**
  ils **dorment**

IMPERFECT
  je **dormais**
  tu **dormais**
  il **dormait**
  nous **dormions**
  vous **dormiez**
  ils **dormaient**

FUTURE
  je dormirai
  tu dormiras
  il dormira
  nous dormirons
  vous dormirez
  ils dormiront

CONDITIONAL
  je dormirais
  tu dormirais
  il dormirait
  nous dormirions
  vous dormiriez
  ils dormiraient

PRESENT SUBJUNCTIVE
  je **dorme**
  tu **dormes**
  il **dorme**
  nous **dormions**
  vous **dormiez**
  ils **dorment**

PAST HISTORIC
  je dormis
  tu dormis
  il dormit
  nous dormîmes
  vous dormîtes
  ils dormirent

écrire *to write*   Auxiliary: **avoir**

PAST PARTICIPLE	IMPERATIVE
écrit	écris
	écrivons
PRESENT PARTICIPLE	**écrivez**
écrivant	

PRESENT	IMPERFECT
j'écris	**j'écrivais**
tu écris	**tu écrivais**
il écrit	**il écrivait**
nous écrivons	**nous écrivions**
vous écrivez	**vous écriviez**
ils écrivent	**ils écrivaient**

FUTURE	CONDITIONAL
j'écrirai	j'écrirais
tu écriras	tu écrirais
il écrira	il écrirait
nous écrirons	nous écririons
vous écrirez	vous écririez
ils écriront	ils écriraient

PRESENT SUBJUNCTIVE	PAST HISTORIC
j'écrive	**j'écrivis**
tu écrives	**tu écrivis**
il écrive	**il écrivit**
nous écrivions	**nous écrivîmes**
vous écriviez	**vous écrivîtes**
ils écrivent	**ils écrivirent**

envoyer *to send*   Auxiliary: **avoir**

PAST PARTICIPLE
envoyé

PRESENT PARTICIPLE
envoyant

IMPERATIVE
envoie
envoyons
envoyez

PRESENT
j'envoie
tu envoies
il envoie
nous envoyons
vous envoyez
ils envoient

IMPERFECT
j'envoyais
tu envoyais
il envoyait
nous envoyions
vous envoyiez
ils envoyaient

FUTURE
j'enverrai
tu enverras
il enverra
nous enverrons
vous enverrez
ils enverront

CONDITIONAL
j'enverrais
tu enverrais
il enverrait
nous enverrions
vous enverriez
ils enverraient

PRESENT SUBJUNCTIVE
j'envoie
tu envoies
il envoie
nous envoyions
vous envoyiez
ils envoient

PAST HISTORIC
j'envoyai
tu envoyas
il envoya
nous envoyâmes
vous envoyâtes
ils envoyèrent

être *to be*   Auxiliary: **avoir**

PAST PARTICIPLE
été

IMPERATIVE
sois
soyons
soyez

PRESENT PARTICIPLE
étant

PRESENT	IMPERFECT
je **suis**	j'**étais**
tu **es**	tu **étais**
il **est**	il **était**
nous **sommes**	nous **étions**
vous **êtes**	vous **étiez**
ils **sont**	ils **étaient**

FUTURE	CONDITIONAL
je **serai**	je **serais**
tu **seras**	tu **serais**
il **sera**	il **serait**
nous **serons**	nous **serions**
vous **serez**	vous **seriez**
ils **seront**	ils **seraient**

PRESENT SUBJUNCTIVE	PAST HISTORIC
je **sois**	je **fus**
tu **sois**	tu **fus**
il **soit**	il **fut**
nous **soyons**	nous **fûmes**
vous **soyez**	vous **fûtes**
ils **soient**	ils **furent**

faire *to do; to make*   Auxiliary: **avoir**

PAST PARTICIPLE
fait

PRESENT PARTICIPLE
faisant

IMPERATIVE
fais
faisons
faites

PRESENT
   je fais
   tu fais
   il fait
  nous faisons
  vous faites
   ils font

IMPERFECT
   je faisais
   tu faisais
   il faisait
  nous faisions
  vous faisiez
   ils faisaient

FUTURE
   je ferai
   tu feras
   il fera
  nous ferons
  vous ferez
   ils feront

CONDITIONAL
   je ferais
   tu ferais
   il ferait
  nous ferions
  vous feriez
   ils feraient

PRESENT SUBJUNCTIVE
   je fasse
   tu fasses
   il fasse
  nous fassions
  vous fassiez
   ils fassent

PAST HISTORIC
   je fis
   tu fis
   il fit
  nous fîmes
  vous fîtes
   ils firent

---

falloir *to be necessary*   Auxiliary: **avoir**

PAST PARTICIPLE
fallu

IMPERATIVE
not used

PRESENT PARTICIPLE
not used

PRESENT **il faut**	IMPERFECT **il fallait**
FUTURE **il faudra**	CONDITIONAL **il faudrait**
PRESENT SUBJUNCTIVE **il faille**	PAST HISTORIC **il fallut**

fuir *to flee* Auxiliary: **avoir**

PAST PARTICIPLE
fui

IMPERATIVE
fuis
fuyons
fuyez

PRESENT PARTICIPLE
fuyant

PRESENT
je fuis
tu fuis
il fuit
nous fuyons
vous fuyez
ils fuient

IMPERFECT
je fuyais
tu fuyais
il fuyait
nous fuyions
vous fuyiez
ils fuyaient

FUTURE
je fuirai
tu fuiras
il fuira
nous fuirons
vous fuirez
ils fuiront

CONDITIONAL
je fuirais
tu fuirais
il fuirait
nous fuirions
vous fuiriez
ils fuiraient

PRESENT SUBJUNCTIVE
je fuie
tu fuies
il fuie
nous fuyions
vous fuyiez
ils fuient

PAST HISTORIC
je fuis
tu fuis
il fuit
nous fuîmes
vous fuîtes
ils fuirent

haïr *to hate*　　　　　　Auxiliary: **avoir**

PAST PARTICIPLE
haï

PRESENT PARTICIPLE
haïssant

IMPERATIVE
hais
haïssons
haïssez

PRESENT	IMPERFECT
je hais	**je haïssais**
tu hais	**tu haïssais**
il hait	**il haïssait**
nous haïssons	**nous haïssions**
vous haïssez	**vous haïssiez**
ils haïssent	**ils haïssaient**

FUTURE	CONDITIONAL
je haïrai	je haïrais
tu haïras	tu haïrais
il haïra	il haïrait
nous haïrons	nous haïrions
vous haïrez	vous haïriez
ils haïront	ils haïraient

PRESENT SUBJUNCTIVE	PAST HISTORIC
je haïsse	**je haïs**
tu haïsses	**tu haïs**
il haïsse	**il haït**
nous haïssions	**nous haïmes**
vous haïssiez	**vous haïtes**
ils haïssent	**ils haïrent**

lire *to read*   Auxiliary: **avoir**

PAST PARTICIPLE	IMPERATIVE
lu	lis
	lisons
PRESENT PARTICIPLE	**lisez**
lisant	

PRESENT	IMPERFECT
je lis	**je lisais**
tu lis	**tu lisais**
il lit	**il lisait**
nous lisons	**nous lisions**
vous lisez	**vous lisiez**
ils lisent	**ils lisaient**

FUTURE	CONDITIONAL
je lirai	je lirais
tu liras	tu lirais
il lira	il lirait
nous lirons	nous lirions
vous lirez	vous liriez
ils liront	ils liraient

PRESENT SUBJUNCTIVE	PAST HISTORIC
je lise	**je lus**
tu lises	**tu lus**
il lise	**il lut**
nous lisions	**nous lûmes**
vous lisiez	**vous lûtes**
ils lisent	**ils lurent**

mettre *to put*   Auxiliary: **avoir**

PAST PARTICIPLE
mis

IMPERATIVE
mets
mettons
mettez

PRESENT PARTICIPLE
mettant

PRESENT
    je **mets**
    tu **mets**
    il **met**
nous mettons
vous mettez
  ils mettent

IMPERFECT
    je mettais
    tu mettais
    il mettait
nous mettions
vous mettiez
  ils mettaient

FUTURE
    je mettrai
    tu mettras
    il mettra
nous mettrons
vous mettrez
  ils mettront

CONDITIONAL
    je mettrais
    tu mettrais
    il mettrait
nous mettrions
vous mettriez
  ils mettraient

PRESENT SUBJUNCTIVE
    je mette
    tu mettes
    il mette
nous mettions
vous mettiez
  ils mettent

PAST HISTORIC
    je **mis**
    tu **mis**
    il **mit**
nous **mîmes**
vous **mîtes**
  ils **mirent**

moudre *to grind* Auxiliary: **avoir**

PAST PARTICIPLE
moulu

PRESENT PARTICIPLE
moulant

IMPERATIVE
mouds
moulons
moulez

PRESENT
je mouds
tu mouds
il moud
nous moulons
vous moulez
ils moulent

IMPERFECT
je moulais
tu moulais
il moulait
nous moulions
vous mouliez
ils moulaient

FUTURE
je moudrai
tu moudras
il moudra
nous moudrons
vous moudrez
ils moudront

CONDITIONAL
je moudrais
tu moudrais
il moudrait
nous moudrions
vous moudriez
ils moudraient

PRESENT SUBJUNCTIVE
je moule
tu moules
il moule
nous moulions
vous mouliez
ils moulent

PAST HISTORIC
je moulus
tu moulus
il moulut
nous moulûmes
vous moulûtes
ils moulurent

mourir *to die*   Auxiliary: **être**

PAST PARTICIPLE
  mort

PRESENT PARTICIPLE
  mourant

IMPERATIVE
  meurs
  mourons
  mourez

PRESENT	IMPERFECT
je **meurs**	je **mourais**
tu **meurs**	tu **mourais**
il **meurt**	il **mourait**
nous **mourons**	nous **mourions**
vous **mourez**	vous **mouriez**
ils **meurent**	ils **mouraient**

FUTURE	CONDITIONAL
je **mourrai**	je **mourrais**
tu **mourras**	tu **mourrais**
il **mourra**	il **mourrait**
nous **mourrons**	nous **mourrions**
vous **mourrez**	vous **mourriez**
ils **mourront**	ils **mourraient**

PRESENT SUBJUNCTIVE	PAST HISTORIC
je **meure**	je **mourus**
tu **meures**	tu **mourus**
il **meure**	il **mourut**
nous **mourions**	nous **mourûmes**
vous **mouriez**	vous **mourûtes**
ils **meurent**	ils **moururent**

naître *to be born*   Auxiliary: **être**

PAST PARTICIPLE	IMPERATIVE
né	**nais**
	naissons
PRESENT PARTICIPLE	**naissez**
naissant	

PRESENT	IMPERFECT
je **nais**	je **naissais**
tu **nais**	tu **naissais**
il **naît**	il **naissait**
nous **naissons**	nous **naissions**
vous **naissez**	vous **naissiez**
ils **naissent**	ils **naissaient**

FUTURE	CONDITIONAL
je naîtrai	je naîtrais
tu naîtras	tu naîtrais
il naîtra	il naîtrait
nous naîtrons	nous naîtrions
vous naîtrez	vous naîtriez
ils naîtront	ils naîtraient

PRESENT SUBJUNCTIVE	PAST HISTORIC
je **naisse**	je **naquis**
tu **naisses**	tu **naquis**
il **naisse**	il **naquit**
nous **naissions**	nous **naquîmes**
vous **naissiez**	vous **naquîtes**
ils **naissent**	ils **naquirent**

ouvrir *to open*   Auxiliary: **avoir**

PAST PARTICIPLE
ouvert

PRESENT PARTICIPLE
ouvrant

IMPERATIVE
ouvre
ouvrons
ouvrez

PRESENT	IMPERFECT
j'ouvre	j'ouvrais
tu ouvres	tu ouvrais
il ouvre	il ouvrait
nous ouvrons	nous ouvrions
vous ouvrez	vous ouvriez
ils ouvrent	ils ouvraient

FUTURE	CONDITIONAL
j'ouvrirai	j'ouvrirais
tu ouvriras	tu ouvrirais
il ouvrira	il ouvrirait
nous ouvrirons	nous ouvririons
vous ouvrirez	vous ouvririez
ils ouvriront	ils ouvriraient

PRESENT SUBJUNCTIVE	PAST HISTORIC
j'ouvre	j'ouvris
tu ouvres	tu ouvris
il ouvre	il ouvrit
nous ouvrions	nous ouvrîmes
vous ouvriez	vous ouvrîtes
ils ouvrent	ils ouvrirent

offrir *to offer*, **souffrir** *to suffer* are conjugated similarly

paraître *to appear*   Auxiliary: **avoir**

PAST PARTICIPLE
paru

IMPERATIVE
parais
paraissons
paraissez

PRESENT PARTICIPLE
paraissant

PRESENT	IMPERFECT
je **parais**	je **paraissais**
tu **parais**	tu **paraissais**
il **paraît**	il **paraissait**
nous **paraissons**	nous **paraissions**
vous **paraissez**	vous **paraissiez**
ils **paraissent**	ils **paraissaient**

FUTURE	CONDITIONAL
je paraîtrai	je paraîtrais
tu paraîtras	tu paraîtrais
il paraîtra	il paraîtrait
nous paraîtrons	nous paraîtrions
vous paraîtrez	vous paraîtriez
ils paraîtront	ils paraîtraient

PRESENT SUBJUNCTIVE	PAST HISTORIC
je **paraisse**	je **parus**
tu **paraisses**	tu **parus**
il **paraisse**	il **parut**
nous **paraissions**	nous **parûmes**
vous **paraissiez**	vous **parûtes**
ils **paraissent**	ils **parurent**

partir *to leave*　　　　　Auxiliary: **être**

PAST PARTICIPLE
parti

PRESENT PARTICIPLE
partant

IMPERATIVE
pars
partons
partez

PRESENT
　je **pars**
　tu **pars**
　il **part**
　nous **partons**
　vous **partez**
　ils **partent**

IMPERFECT
　je **partais**
　tu **partais**
　il **partait**
　nous **partions**
　vous **partiez**
　ils **partaient**

FUTURE
　je partirai
　tu partiras
　il partira
　nous partirons
　vous partirez
　ils partiront

CONDITIONAL
　je partirais
　tu partirais
　il partirait
　nous partirions
　vous partiriez
　ils partiraient

PRESENT SUBJUNCTIVE
　je **parte**
　tu **partes**
　il **parte**
　nous **partions**
　vous **partiez**
　ils **partent**

PAST HISTORIC
　je partis
　tu partis
　il partit
　nous partîmes
　vous partîtes
　ils partirent

plaire *to please*   Auxiliary: **avoir**

PAST PARTICIPLE
plu

IMPERATIVE
plais
plaisons
plaisez

PRESENT PARTICIPLE
plaisant

PRESENT	IMPERFECT
je plais	**je plaisais**
tu plais	**tu plaisais**
il plaît	**il plaisait**
nous plaisons	**nous plaisions**
vous plaisez	**vous plaisiez**
ils plaisent	**ils plaisaient**

FUTURE	CONDITIONAL
je plairai	je plairais
tu plairas	tu plairais
il plaira	il plairait
nous plairons	nous plairions
vous plairez	vous plairiez
ils plairont	ils plairaient

PRESENT SUBJUNCTIVE	PAST HISTORIC
je plaise	**je plus**
tu plaises	**tu plus**
il plaise	**il plut**
nous plaisions	**nous plûmes**
vous plaisiez	**vous plûtes**
ils plaisent	**ils plurent**

pleuvoir *to rain*   Auxiliary: **avoir**

PAST PARTICIPLE
plu

IMPERATIVE
not used

PRESENT PARTICIPLE
pleuvant

PRESENT
il pleut

IMPERFECT
il pleuvait

FUTURE
il pleuvra

CONDITIONAL
il pleuvrait

PRESENT SUBJUNCTIVE
il pleuve

PAST HISTORIC
il plut

pouvoir *to be able to*   Auxiliary: **avoir**

PAST PARTICIPLE
pu

IMPERATIVE
not used

PRESENT PARTICIPLE
pouvant

PRESENT	IMPERFECT
je **peux***	je **pouvais**
tu **peux**	tu **pouvais**
il **peut**	il **pouvait**
nous **pouvons**	nous **pouvions**
vous **pouvez**	vous **pouviez**
ils **peuvent**	ils **pouvaient**

FUTURE	CONDITIONAL
je **pourrai**	je **pourrais**
tu **pourras**	tu **pourrais**
il **pourra**	il **pourrait**
nous **pourrons**	nous **pourrions**
vous **pourrez**	vous **pourriez**
ils **pourront**	ils **pourraient**

PRESENT SUBJUNCTIVE	PAST HISTORIC
je **puisse**	je **pus**
tu **puisses**	tu **pus**
il **puisse**	il **put**
nous **puissions**	nous **pûmes**
vous **puissiez**	vous **pûtes**
ils **puissent**	ils **purent**

In questions: **puis-je?**

prendre *to take* Auxiliary: **avoir**

PAST PARTICIPLE
pris

PRESENT PARTICIPLE
prenant

IMPERATIVE
prends
prenons
prenez

PRESENT	IMPERFECT
je prends	**je prenais**
tu prends	**tu prenais**
il prend	**il prenait**
nous prenons	**nous prenions**
vous prenez	**vous preniez**
ils prennent	**ils prenaient**

FUTURE	CONDITIONAL
je prendrai	je prendrais
tu prendras	tu prendrais
il prendra	il prendrait
nous prendrons	nous prendrions
vous prendrez	vous prendriez
ils prendront	ils prendraient

PRESENT SUBJUNCTIVE	PAST HISTORIC
je prenne	**je pris**
tu prennes	**tu pris**
il prenne	**il prit**
nous prenions	**nous prîmes**
vous preniez	**vous prîtes**
ils prennent	**ils prirent**

recevoir to receive   Auxiliary: **avoir**

PAST PARTICIPLE
  reçu

PRESENT PARTICIPLE
  recevant

IMPERATIVE
  reçois
  recevons
  recevez

PRESENT
  je **reçois**
  tu **reçois**
  il **reçoit**
  nous **recevons**
  vous **recevez**
  ils **reçoivent**

IMPERFECT
  je **recevais**
  tu **recevais**
  il **recevait**
  nous **recevions**
  vous **receviez**
  ils **recevaient**

FUTURE
  je **recevrai**
  tu **recevras**
  il **recevra**
  nous **recevrons**
  vous **recevrez**
  ils **recevront**

CONDITIONAL
  je **recevrais**
  tu **recevrais**
  il **recevrait**
  nous **recevrions**
  vous **recevriez**
  ils **recevraient**

PRESENT SUBJUNCTIVE
  je **reçoive**
  tu **reçoives**
  il **reçoive**
  nous **recevions**
  vous **receviez**
  ils **reçoivent**

PAST HISTORIC
  je **reçus**
  tu **reçus**
  il **reçut**
  nous **reçûmes**
  vous **reçûtes**
  ils **reçurent**

résoudre *to solve*   Auxiliary: **avoir**

PAST PARTICIPLE
résolu

PRESENT PARTICIPLE
résolvant

IMPERATIVE
résous
résolvons
résolvez

PRESENT	IMPERFECT
je **résous**	je **résolvais**
tu **résous**	tu **résolvais**
il **résout**	il **résolvait**
nous **résolvons**	nous **résolvions**
vous **résolvez**	vous **résolviez**
ils **résolvent**	ils **résolvaient**

FUTURE	CONDITIONAL
je **résoudrai**	je **résoudrais**
tu **résoudras**	tu **résoudrais**
il **résoudra**	il **résoudrait**
nous **résoudrons**	nous **résoudrions**
vous **résoudrez**	vous **résoudriez**
ils **résoudront**	ils **résoudraient**

PRESENT SUBJUNCTIVE	PAST HISTORIC
je **résolve**	je **résolus**
tu **résolves**	tu **résolus**
il **résolve**	il **résolut**
nous **résolvions**	nous **résolûmes**
vous **résolviez**	vous **résolûtes**
ils **résolvent**	ils **résolurent**

rire to laugh   Auxiliary: **avoir**

PAST PARTICIPLE	IMPERATIVE
ri	ris
	rions
PRESENT PARTICIPLE	riez
riant	

PRESENT	IMPERFECT
je ris	je riais
tu ris	tu riais
il rit	il riait
nous rions	nous riions
vous riez	vous riiez
ils rient	ils riaient

FUTURE	CONDITIONAL
je rirai	je rirais
tu riras	tu rirais
il rira	il rirait
nous rirons	nous ririons
vous rirez	vous ririez
ils riront	ils riraient

PRESENT SUBJUNCTIVE	PAST HISTORIC
je rie	**je ris**
tu ries	**tu ris**
il rie	**il rit**
nous riions	**nous rîmes**
vous riiez	**vous rîtes**
ils rient	**ils rirent**

rompre *to break*   Auxiliary: **avoir**

PAST PARTICIPLE
rompu

PRESENT PARTICIPLE
rompant

IMPERATIVE
romps
rompons
rompez

PRESENT
  je romps
  tu romps
  il rompt
  nous rompons
  vous rompez
  ils rompent

IMPERFECT
  je rompais
  tu rompais
  il rompait
  nous rompions
  vous rompiez
  ils rompaient

FUTURE
  je romprai
  tu rompras
  il rompra
  nous romprons
  vous romprez
  ils rompront

CONDITIONAL
  je romprais
  tu romprais
  il romprait
  nous romprions
  vous rompriez
  ils rompraient

PRESENT SUBJUNCTIVE
  je rompe
  tu rompes
  il rompe
  nous rompions
  vous rompiez
  ils rompent

PAST HISTORIC
  je rompis
  tu rompis
  il rompit
  nous rompîmes
  vous rompîtes
  ils rompirent

savoir *to know*   Auxiliary: **avoir**

PAST PARTICIPLE
  su

IMPERATIVE
  sache
  sachons
  sachez

PRESENT PARTICIPLE
  sachant

PRESENT	IMPERFECT
je **sais**	je **savais**
tu **sais**	tu **savais**
il **sait**	il **savait**
nous **savons**	nous **savions**
vous **savez**	vous **saviez**
ils **savent**	ils **savaient**

FUTURE	CONDITIONAL
je **saurai**	je **saurais**
tu **sauras**	tu **saurais**
il **saura**	il **saurait**
nous **saurons**	nous **saurions**
vous **saurez**	vous **sauriez**
ils **sauront**	ils **sauraient**

PRESENT SUBJUNCTIVE	PAST HISTORIC
je **sache**	je **sus**
tu **saches**	tu **sus**
il **sache**	il **sut**
nous **sachions**	nous **sûmes**
vous **sachiez**	vous **sûtes**
ils **sachent**	ils **surent**

sentir *to feel; to smell*   Auxiliary: **avoir**

PAST PARTICIPLE
senti

PRESENT PARTICIPLE
sentant

IMPERATIVE
sens
sentons
sentez

PRESENT
  je sens
  tu sens
  il sent
  nous sentons
  vous sentez
  ils sentent

IMPERFECT
  je sentais
  tu sentais
  il sentait
  nous sentions
  vous sentiez
  ils sentaient

FUTURE
  je sentirai
  tu sentiras
  il sentira
  nous sentirons
  vous sentirez
  ils sentiront

CONDITIONAL
  je sentirais
  tu sentirais
  il sentirait
  nous sentirions
  vous sentiriez
  ils sentiraient

PRESENT SUBJUNCTIVE
  je sente
  tu sentes
  il sente
  nous sentions
  vous sentiez
  ils sentent

PAST HISTORIC
  je sentis
  tu sentis
  il sentit
  nous sentîmes
  vous sentîtes
  ils sentirent

servir *to serve*   Auxiliary: **avoir**

PAST PARTICIPLE
servi

PRESENT PARTICIPLE
servant

IMPERATIVE
sers
servons
servez

PRESENT
  je sers
  tu sers
  il sert
  nous servons
  vous servez
  ils servent

FUTURE
  je servirai
  tu serviras
  il servira
  nous servirons
  vous servirez
  ils serviront

PRESENT SUBJUNCTIVE
  je serve
  tu serves
  il serve
  nous servions
  vous serviez
  ils servent

IMPERFECT
  je servais
  tu servais
  il servait
  nous servions
  vous serviez
  ils servaient

CONDITIONAL
  je servirais
  tu servirais
  il servirait
  nous servirions
  vous serviriez
  ils serviraient

PAST HISTORIC
  je servis
  tu servis
  il servit
  nous servîmes
  vous servîtes
  ils servirent

sortir to go/come out   Auxiliary: **être**

PAST PARTICIPLE
sorti

PRESENT PARTICIPLE
sortant

IMPERATIVE
sors
sortons
sortez

PRESENT	IMPERFECT
je **sors**	je **sortais**
tu **sors**	tu **sortais**
il **sort**	il **sortait**
nous **sortons**	nous **sortions**
vous **sortez**	vous **sortiez**
ils **sortent**	ils **sortaient**

FUTURE	CONDITIONAL
je sortirai	je sortirais
tu sortiras	tu sortirais
il sortira	il sortirait
nous sortirons	nous sortirions
vous sortirez	vous sortiriez
ils sortiront	ils sortiraient

PRESENT SUBJUNCTIVE	PAST HISTORIC
je **sorte**	je sortis
tu **sortes**	tu sortis
il **sorte**	il sortit
nous **sortions**	nous sortîmes
vous **sortiez**	vous sortîtes
ils **sortent**	ils sortirent

suffire *to be enough* Auxiliary: **avoir**

PAST PARTICIPLE
suffi

IMPERATIVE
suffis
suffisons
suffisez

PRESENT PARTICIPLE
suffisant

PRESENT
je suffis
tu suffis
il suffit
nous suffisons
vous suffisez
ils suffisent

IMPERFECT
je **suffisais**
tu **suffisais**
il **suffisait**
nous **suffisions**
vous **suffisiez**
ils **suffisaient**

FUTURE
je suffirai
tu suffiras
il suffira
nous suffirons
vous suffirez
ils suffiront

CONDITIONAL
je suffirais
tu suffirais
il suffirait
nous suffirions
vous suffiriez
ils suffiraient

PRESENT SUBJUNCTIVE
je **suffise**
tu **suffises**
il **suffise**
nous **suffisions**
vous **suffisiez**
ils **suffisent**

PAST HISTORIC
je **suffis**
tu **suffis**
il **suffit**
nous **suffîmes**
vous **suffîtes**
ils **suffirent**

suivre *to follow* | Auxiliary: **avoir**

PAST PARTICIPLE	IMPERATIVE
suivi	**suis**
	suivons
PRESENT PARTICIPLE	suivez
suivant	

PRESENT	IMPERFECT
je suis	je suivais
tu suis	tu suivais
il suit	il suivait
nous suivons	nous suivions
vous suivez	vous suiviez
ils suivent	ils suivaient

FUTURE	CONDITIONAL
je suivrai	je suivrais
tu suivras	tu suivrais
il suivra	il suivrait
nous suivrons	nous suivrions
vous suivrez	vous suivriez
ils suivront	ils suivraient

PRESENT SUBJUNCTIVE	PAST HISTORIC
je suive	je suivis
tu suives	tu suivis
il suive	il suivit
nous suivions	nous suivîmes
vous suiviez	vous suivîtes
ils suivent	ils suivirent

se taire *to stop talking*   Auxiliary: être

PAST PARTICIPLE
tu

IMPERATIVE
tais-toi
taisons-nous
taisez-vous

PRESENT PARTICIPLE
se taisant

PRESENT
je me tais
tu te tais
il se tait
nous nous taisons
vous vous taisez
ils se taisent

IMPERFECT
je me taisais
tu te taisais
il se taisait
nous nous taisions
vous vous taisiez
ils se taisaient

FUTURE
je me tairai
tu te tairas
il se taira
nous nous tairons
vous vous tairez
ils se tairont

CONDITIONAL
je me tairais
tu te tairais
il se tairait
nous nous tairions
vous vous tairiez
ils se tairaient

PRESENT SUBJUNCTIVE
je me taise
tu te taises
il se taise
nous nous taisions
vous vous taisiez
ils se taisent

PAST HISTORIC
je me tus
tu te tus
il se tut
nous nous tûmes
vous vous tûtes
ils se turent

tenir *to hold*   Auxiliary: **avoir**

PAST PARTICIPLE
tenu

PRESENT PARTICIPLE
tenant

IMPERATIVE
tiens
tenons
tenez

PRESENT	IMPERFECT
je **tiens**	je **tenais**
tu **tiens**	tu **tenais**
il **tient**	il **tenait**
nous **tenons**	nous **tenions**
vous **tenez**	vous **teniez**
ils **tiennent**	ils **tenaient**

FUTURE	CONDITIONAL
je **tiendrai**	je **tiendrais**
tu **tiendras**	tu **tiendrais**
il **tiendra**	il **tiendrait**
nous **tiendrons**	nous **tiendrions**
vous **tiendrez**	vous **tiendriez**
ils **tiendront**	ils **tiendraient**

PRESENT SUBJUNCTIVE	PAST HISTORIC
je **tienne**	je **tins**
tu **tiennes**	tu **tins**
il **tienne**	il **tint**
nous **tenions**	nous **tînmes**
vous **teniez**	vous **tîntes**
ils **tiennent**	ils **tinrent**

vaincre *to defeat* Auxiliary: **avoir**

PAST PARTICIPLE	IMPERATIVE
vaincu	vaincs
	vainquons
PRESENT PARTICIPLE	**vainquez**
vainquant	

PRESENT	IMPERFECT
je vaincs	**je vainquais**
tu vaincs	**tu vainquais**
il vainc	**il vainquait**
nous vainquons	**nous vainquions**
vous vainquez	**vous vainquiez**
ils vainquent	**ils vainquaient**

FUTURE	CONDITIONAL
je vaincrai	je vaincrais
tu vaincras	tu vaincrais
il vaincra	il vaincrait
nous vaincrons	nous vaincrions
vous vaincrez	vous vaincriez
ils vaincront	ils vaincraient

PRESENT SUBJUNCTIVE	PAST HISTORIC
je vainque	**je vainquis**
tu vainques	**tu vainquis**
il vainque	**il vainquit**
nous vainquions	**nous vainquîmes**
vous vainquiez	**vous vainquîtes**
ils vainquent	**ils vainquirent**

valoir *to be worth*   Auxiliary: **avoir**

PAST PARTICIPLE
valu

PRESENT PARTICIPLE
valant

IMPERATIVE
vaux
valons
valez

PRESENT
je **vaux**
tu **vaux**
il **vaut**
nous **valons**
vous **valez**
ils **valent**

IMPERFECT
je **valais**
tu **valais**
il **valait**
nous **valions**
vous **valiez**
ils **valaient**

FUTURE
je **vaudrai**
tu **vaudras**
il **vaudra**
nous **vaudrons**
vous **vaudrez**
ils **vaudront**

CONDITIONAL
je **vaudrais**
tu **vaudrais**
il **vaudrait**
nous **vaudrions**
vous **vaudriez**
ils **vaudraient**

PRESENT SUBJUNCTIVE
je **vaille**
tu **vailles**
il **vaille**
nous **valions**
vous **valiez**
ils **vaillent**

PAST HISTORIC
je **valus**
tu **valus**
il **valut**
nous **valûmes**
vous **valûtes**
ils **valurent**

venir *to come*   Auxiliary: **être**

PAST PARTICIPLE
  venu

PRESENT PARTICIPLE
  venant

IMPERATIVE
  viens
  venons
  venez

PRESENT	IMPERFECT
je viens	je venais
tu viens	tu venais
il vient	il venait
nous venons	nous venions
vous venez	vous veniez
ils viennent	ils venaient

FUTURE	CONDITIONAL
je viendrai	je viendrais
tu viendras	tu viendrais
il viendra	il viendrait
nous viendrons	nous viendrions
vous viendrez	vous viendriez
ils viendront	ils viendraient

PRESENT SUBJUNCTIVE	PAST HISTORIC
je vienne	je vins
tu viennes	tu vins
il vienne	il vint
nous venions	nous vînmes
vous veniez	vous vîntes
ils viennent	ils vinrent

vêtir *to dress*   Auxiliary: **avoir**

PAST PARTICIPLE	IMPERATIVE
vêtu	**vêts**
	vêtons
PRESENT PARTICIPLE	**vêtez**
vêtant	

PRESENT	IMPERFECT
je **vêts**	je **vêtais**
tu **vêts**	tu **vêtais**
il **vêt**	il **vêtait**
nous **vêtons**	nous **vêtions**
vous **vêtez**	vous **vêtiez**
ils **vêtent**	ils **vêtaient**

FUTURE	CONDITIONAL
je vêtirai	je vêtirais
tu vêtiras	tu vêtirais
il vêtira	il vêtirait
nous vêtirons	nous vêtirions
vous vêtirez	vous vêtiriez
ils vêtiront	ils vêtiraient

PRESENT SUBJUNCTIVE	PAST HISTORIC
je **vête**	je vêtis
tu **vêtes**	tu vêtis
il **vête**	il vêtit
nous **vêtions**	nous vêtîmes
vous **vêtiez**	vous vêtîtes
ils **vêtent**	ils vêtirent

vivre *to live* Auxiliary: **avoir**

PAST PARTICIPLE
vécu

IMPERATIVE
vis
vivons
vivez

PRESENT PARTICIPLE
vivant

PRESENT	IMPERFECT
je **vis**	je vivais
tu **vis**	tu vivais
il **vit**	il vivait
nous vivons	nous vivions
vous vivez	vous viviez
ils vivent	ils vivaient

FUTURE	CONDITIONAL
je vivrai	je vivrais
tu vivras	tu vivrais
il vivra	il vivrait
nous vivrons	nous vivrions
vous vivrez	vous vivriez
ils vivront	ils vivraient

PRESENT SUBJUNCTIVE	PAST HISTORIC
je vive	je **vécus**
tu vives	tu **vécus**
il vive	il **vécut**
nous vivions	nous **vécûmes**
vous viviez	vous **vécûtes**
ils vivent	ils **vécurent**

voir *to see*   Auxiliary: **avoir**

PAST PARTICIPLE	IMPERATIVE
vu	**vois**
	voyons
PRESENT PARTICIPLE	**voyez**
voyant	

PRESENT

   je **vois**
   tu **vois**
   il **voit**
   nous **voyons**
   vous **voyez**
   ils **voient**

IMPERFECT

   je **voyais**
   tu **voyais**
   il **voyait**
   nous **voyions**
   vous **voyiez**
   ils **voyaient**

FUTURE

   je **verrai**
   tu **verras**
   il **verra**
   nous **verrons**
   vous **verrez**
   ils **verront**

CONDITIONAL

   je **verrais**
   tu **verrais**
   il **verrait**
   nous **verrions**
   vous **verriez**
   ils **verraient**

PRESENT SUBJUNCTIVE

   je **voie**
   tu **voies**
   il **voie**
   nous **voyions**
   vous **voyiez**
   ils **voient**

PAST HISTORIC

   je **vis**
   tu **vis**
   il **vit**
   nous **vîmes**
   vous **vîtes**
   ils **virent**

vouloir *to wish, want*   Auxiliary: **avoir**

PAST PARTICIPLE
voulu

PRESENT PARTICIPLE
voulant

IMPERATIVE
veuille
veuillons
veuillez

PRESENT
je **veux**
tu **veux**
il **veut**
nous **voulons**
vous **voulez**
ils **veulent**

IMPERFECT
je **voulais**
tu **voulais**
il **voulait**
nous **voulions**
vous **vouliez**
ils **voulaient**

FUTURE
je **voudrai**
tu **voudras**
il **voudra**
nous **voudrons**
vous **voudrez**
ils **voudront**

CONDITIONAL
je **voudrais**
tu **voudrais**
il **voudrait**
nous **voudrions**
vous **voudriez**
ils **voudraient**

PRESENT SUBJUNCTIVE
je **veuille**
tu **veuilles**
il **veuille**
nous **voulions**
vous **vouliez**
ils **veuillent**

PAST HISTORIC
je **voulus**
tu **voulus**
il **voulut**
nous **voulûmes**
vous **voulûtes**
ils **voulurent**

The Gender of Nouns

In French, all nouns are either masculine or feminine, whether denoting people, animals or things. Unlike English, there is no neuter gender for inanimate objects and abstract nouns.

Gender is largely unpredictable and has to be learnt for each noun. However, the following guidelines will help you determine the gender for certain types of nouns.

- Nouns denoting male people and animals are usually – but not always – masculine, e.g.

  un homme   **un taureau**
  a man   *a bull*
  un infirmier   **un porc**
  a (male) nurse   *a pig*

- Nouns denoting female people and animals are usually – but not always – feminine, e.g.

  une fille   **une vache**
  a girl   *a cow*
  une infirmière   **une truie**
  a nurse   *a sow*

- Some nouns are masculine OR feminine depending on the sex of the person to whom they refer, e.g.

  un camarade   **une camarade**
  a (male) friend   *a (female) friend*
  un Belge   **une Belge**
  a Belgian (man)   *a Belgian (woman)*

- Other nouns referring to either men or women have only one gender which applies to both, e.g.

  un professeur   **une personne**   **une sentinelle**
  a teacher   *a person*   *a sentry*
  un témoin   **une victime**   **une recrue**
  a witness   *a victim*   *a recruit*

- Sometimes the ending of the noun indicates its gender. Shown below are some of the most important to guide you:

Masculine endings

-age	le courage *courage*, le rinçage *rinsing*
	EXCEPTIONS: une cage *a cage*, une image *a picture*, la nage *swimming*, une page *a page*, une plage *a beach*, une rage *a rage*
-ment	le commencement *the beginning*
	EXCEPTION: une jument *a mare*
-oir	un couloir *a corridor*, un miroir *a mirror*
-sme	le pessimisme *pessimism*, l'enthousiasme *enthusiasm*

Feminine endings

-ance, -anse	la confiance *confidence*, la danse *dancing*
-ence, -ense	la prudence *caution*, la défense *defence*
	EXCEPTION: le silence *silence*
-ion	une région *a region*, une addition *a bill*
	EXCEPTIONS: un pion *a pawn*, un espion *a spy*
-oire	une baignoire *a bath(tub)*
-té, -tié	la beauté *beauty*, la moitié *half*

- Suffixes which differentiate between male and female are shown on pp. 134 and 136

- The following words have different meanings depending on gender:

le crêpe	*crêpe*	la crêpe	*pancake*
le livre	*book*	la livre	*pound*
le manche	*handle*	la manche	*sleeve*
le mode	*method*	la mode	*fashion*
le moule	*mould*	la moule	*mussel*
le page	*page(boy)*	la page	*page (in book)*
le physique	*physique*	la physique	*physics*
le poêle	*stove*	la poêle	*frying pan*
le somme	*nap*	la somme	*sum*
le tour	*turn*	la tour	*tower*
le vapeur	*steamship*	la vapeur	*steam*
le voile	*veil*	la voile	*sail*

Gender: the formation of feminines

As in English, male and female are sometimes differentiated by the use of two quite separate words, e.g.

mon oncle	**ma tante**
my uncle	*my aunt*
un taureau	**une vache**
a bull	*a cow*

There are, however, some words in French which show this distinction by the form of their ending

- Some nouns add an **e** to the masculine singular form to form the feminine (→**1**)
- If the masculine singular form already ends in **-e**, no further **e** is added in the feminine (→**2**)
- Some nouns undergo a further change when **e** is added. These changes occur regularly and are shown on p. 136

Feminine forms to note

MASCULINE	FEMININE	
un âne	une ânesse	*donkey*
le comte	la comtesse	*count/countess*
le duc	la duchesse	*duke/duchess*
un Esquimau	une Esquimaude	*Eskimo*
le fou	la folle	*mad man/mad woman*
le Grec	la Grecque	*Greek*
un hôte	une hôtesse	*host/hostess*
le jumeau	la jumelle	*twin*
le maître	la maîtresse	*master/mistress*
le prince	la princesse	*prince/princess*
le tigre	la tigresse	*tiger/tigress*
le traître	la traîtresse	*traitor*
le Turc	la Turque	*Turk*
le vieux	la vieille	*old man/old woman*

Continued

1 **un ami**
a (male) friend
un employé
a (male) employee
un Français
a Frenchman

    une amie
    a (female) friend
    une employée
    a (female) employee
    une Française
    a Frenchwoman

2 **un élève**
a (male) pupil
un collègue
a (male) colleague
un camarade
a (male) friend

    une élève
    a (female) pupil
    une collègue
    a (female) colleague
    une camarade
    a (female) friend

Regular feminine endings

MASC. SING.	FEM. SING.	
-f	-ve	(→1)
-x	-se	(→2)
-eur	-euse	(→3)
-teur	{-teuse	(→4)
	{-trice	(→5)

Some nouns double the final consonant before adding **e**:

MASC. SING.	FEM. SING.	
-an	-anne	(→6)
-en	-enne	(→7)
-on	-onne	(→8)
-et	-ette	(→9)
-el	-elle	(→10)

Some nouns add an accent to the final syllable before adding **e**:

MASC. SING.	FEM. SING.	
-er	-ère	(→11)

Pronunciation and feminine endings

This is dealt with on p. 244.

1 **un Juif**
   a Jew
   un veuf
   a widower

   une Juive
   a Jewish woman
   une veuve
   a widow

2 **un époux**
   a husband
   un amoureux
   a man in love

   une épouse
   a wife
   une amoureuse
   a woman in love

3 **un danseur**
   a dancer
   un voleur
   a thief

   une danseuse
   a dancer
   une voleuse
   a thief

4 **un menteur**
   a liar
   un flatteur
   a flatterer

   une menteuse
   a liar
   une flatteuse
   a flatterer

5 **un acteur**
   an actor
   un conducteur
   a driver

   une actrice
   an actress
   une conductrice
   a (female) driver

6 **un paysan**
   a countryman
   une paysanne
   a countrywoman

7 **un Parisien**
   a Parisian
   une Parisienne
   a Parisian (woman)

8 **un baron**
   a baron
   une baronne
   a baroness

9 **le cadet**
   the youngest (child)
   la cadette
   the youngest (child)

10 **un intellectuel**
   an intellectual
   une intellectuelle
   an intellectual

11 **un étranger**
   a foreigner
   le dernier
   the last (one)
   une étrangère
   a foreigner
   la dernière
   the last (one)

The formation of plurals

- Most nouns add **s** to the singular form (→**1**)

- When the singular form already ends in **-s**, **-x** or **-z**, no further **s** is added (→**2**)

- For nouns ending in **-au**, **-eau** or **-eu**, the plural ends in **-aux**, **-eaux** or **-eux** (→**3**)
  Exceptions: **pneu**   *tyre*   (plur: **pneus**)
              bleu   *bruise*   (plur: **bleus**)

- For nouns ending in **-al** or **-ail**, the plural ends in **-aux** (→**4**)
  Exceptions: **bal**   *ball*   (plur: **bals**)
              festival   *festival* (plur: **festivals**)
              chandail   *sweater*   (plur: **chandails**)
              détail   *detail*   (plur: **détails**)

- Forming the plural of compound nouns is complicated and you are advised to check each one individually in a dictionary

Irregular plural forms

- Some masculine nouns ending in **-ou** add **x** in the plural. These are:
  bijou   *jewel*   **genou**   *knee*   **joujou**   *toy*
  caillou *pebble*   **hibou**   *owl*   **pou**   *louse*
  chou   *cabbage*

- Some other nouns are totally unpredictable. Chief among these are:

SINGULAR		PLURAL
œil	*eye*	yeux
ciel	*sky*	cieux
Monsieur	*Mr.*	Messieurs
Madame	*Mrs.*	Mesdames
Mademoiselle	*Miss*	Mesdemoiselles

Pronunciation of plural forms

This is dealt with on p. 244

1 **le jardin**   **les jardins**
    the garden   the gardens
    une voiture   **des voitures**
    a car   (some) cars
    l'hôtel   **les hôtels**
    the hotel   the hotels

2 **un tas**   **des tas**
    a heap   (some) heaps
    une voix   **des voix**
    a voice   (some) voices
    le gaz   **les gaz**
    the gas   the gases

3 **un Esquimau**   **des Esquimaux**
    an Eskimo   (some) Eskimos
    le chapeau   **les chapeaux**
    the hat   the hats
    le feu   **les feux**
    the fire   the fires

4 **le journal**   **les journaux**
    the newspaper   the newspapers
    un travail   **des travaux**
    a job   (some) jobs

The Definite Article

	WITH MASC. NOUN	WITH FEM. NOUN	
SING.	**le (l')**	**la (l')**	*the*
PLUR.	**les**	**les**	*the*

- The gender and number of the noun determines the form of the article (→**1**)

- **le** and **la** change to **l'** before a vowel or an **h** 'mute' (→**2**)

- For uses of the definite article see p. 142

- **à + le/la (l'), à + les**

	WITH MASC. NOUN	WITH FEM. NOUN	
SING.	**au (à l')**	**à la (à l')**	(→**3**)
PLUR.	**aux**	**aux**	

- The definite article combines with the preposition **à**, as shown above. You should pay particular attention to the masculine singular form **au**, and both plural forms **aux**, since these are not visually the sum of their parts

- **de + le/la (l'), de + les**

	WITH MASC. NOUN	WITH FEM. NOUN	
SING.	**du (de l')**	**de la (de l')**	(→**4**)
PLUR.	**des**	**des**	

- The definite article combines with the preposition **de**, as shown above. You should pay particular attention to the masculine singular form **du**, and both plural forms **des**, since these are not visually the sum of their parts

Continued

MASCULINE	FEMININE
1 le train	la gare
the train	the station
le garçon	la fille
the boy	the girl
les hôtels	les écoles
the hotels	the schools
les professeurs	les femmes
the teachers	the women
2 l'acteur	l'actrice
the actor	the actress
l'effet	l'eau
the effect	the water
l'ingrédient	l'idée
the ingredient	the idea
l'objet	l'ombre
the object	the shadow
l'univers	l'usine
the universe	the factory
l'hôpital	l'heure
the hospital	the time
3 au cinéma	à la bibliothèque
at/to the cinema	at/to the library
à l'employé	à l'infirmière
to the employee	to the nurse
à l'hôpital	à l'hôtesse
at/to the hospital	to the hostess
aux étudiants	aux maisons
to the students	to the houses
4 du bureau	de la réunion
from/of the office	from/of the meeting
de l'auteur	de l'Italienne
from/of the author	from/of the Italian woman
de l'hôte	de l'horloge
from/of the host	of the clock
des Etats-Unis	des vendeuses
from/of the United States	from/of the saleswomen

Uses of the definite article

While the definite article is used in much the same way in French as it is in English, its use is more widespread in French. Unlike English the definite article is also used:

- with abstract nouns, except when following certain prepositions (→1)

- in generalisations, especially with plural or uncountable* nouns (→2)

- with names of countries (→3)
  Exceptions: no article with countries following **en** *to/in* (→4)

- with parts of the body (→5)
  'Ownership' is often indicated by an indirect object pronoun or a reflexive pronoun (→6)

- in expressions of quantity/rate/price (→7)

- with titles/ranks/professions followed by a proper name (→8)

- The definite article is NOT used with nouns in apposition (→9)

*An uncountable noun is one which cannot be used in the plural or with an indefinite article, e.g. **l'acier** *steel*, **le lait** *milk*

1 **Les prix montent**
Prices are rising
L'amour rayonne dans ses yeux
Love shines in his eyes
BUT **avec plaisir   sans espoir**
with pleasure   without hope

2 **Je n'aime pas le café**
I don't like coffee
Les enfants ont besoin d'être aimés
Children need to be loved

3 **le Japon   la France   l'Italie   les Pays-Bas**
Japan   France   Italy   The Netherlands

4 **aller en Espagne**   **Il travaille en Iran**
to go to Spain   He works in Iran

5 **Tournez la tête à gauche**
Turn your head to the left
J'ai mal à la gorge
My throat is sore, I have a sore throat

6 **La tête me tourne**
My head is spinning
Elle s'est brossé les dents
She brushed her teeth

7 **8 francs le mètre/le kilo/la douzaine/la pièce**
8 francs a metre/a kilo/a dozen/each
rouler à 80 km à l'heure
to go at 50 m.p.h.
payé à l'heure/au jour/au mois
paid by the hour/by the day/by the month

8 **le roi Georges III**   **le capitaine Durand**
King George III   Captain Durand
le docteur Courtin   **Monsieur le président**
Dr. Courtin   Mr. Chairman/President

9 **Victor Hugo, grand écrivain du dix-neuvième siècle**
Victor Hugo, a great author of the nineteenth century
Joseph Leblanc, inventeur et entrepreneur, a été le premier ...
Joseph Leblanc, an inventor and entrepreneur, was the first ...

The Partitive Article

The partitive article has the sense of *some* or *any*, although the French is not always translated in English.

Forms of the partitive

	WITH MASC. NOUN	WITH FEM. NOUN	
SING.	**du (de l')**	**de la (de l')**	some, any
PLUR.	**des**	**des**	some, any

- The gender and number of the noun determines the form of the partitive (→**1**)

- The forms shown in brackets are used before a vowel or an **h** 'mute' (→**2**)

- **des** becomes **de** (**d'** + vowel) before an adjective (→**3**), unless the adjective and noun are seen as forming one unit (→**4**)

- In negative sentences **de** (**d'** + vowel) is used for both genders, singular and plural (→**5**)
  Exception: after **ne ... que** *only*, the positive forms above are used (→**6**)

1 Avez-vous du sucre?
Have you any sugar?
J'ai acheté de la farine et de la margarine
I bought (some) flour and margarine
Il a mangé des gâteaux
He ate some cakes
Est-ce qu'il y a des lettres pour moi?
Are there (any) letters for me?

2 Il me doit de l'argent   **C'est de l'histoire ancienne**
He owes me (some) money   That's ancient history

3 Il a fait de gros efforts pour nous aider
He made a great effort to help us
Cette région a de belles églises
This region has some beautiful churches

4 des petits amis   **des jeunes gens**
boyfriends   young people

5 Je n'ai pas de nourriture/d'argent
I don't have any food/money
Vous n'avez pas de souliers/d'œufs?
Have you no shoes/eggs?
Je ne mange jamais de viande/d'omelettes
I never eat meat/omelettes
Il ne veut plus de visiteurs/d'eau
He doesn't want any more visitors/water

6 Il ne boit que du thé/de la bière/de l'eau
He only drinks tea/beer/water
Je n'ai que des souvenirs
I only have memories

The Indefinite Article

	WITH MASC. NOUN	WITH FEM. NOUN	
SING.	**un**	**une**	*a*
PLUR.	**des**	**des**	*some*

- **des** is also the plural of the partitive article (see p. 144)

- In negative sentences, **de** (**d'** + vowel) is used for both singular and plural (→1)

- The indefinite article is used in French largely as it is in English EXCEPT:
    - there is no article when a person's profession is being stated (→2)
    The article *is* present however, following **ce** (**c'** + vowel) (→3)

    - the English article is not translated by **un/une** in constructions like *what a surprise, what an idiot* (→4)

    - in structures of the type given in example **5** the article **un/une** is used in French and not translated in English (→5)

1 **Je n'ai pas de livre/d'enfants**
  I don't have a book/(any) children

2 **Il est professeur**   **Ma mère est infirmière**
  He's a teacher   My mother's a nurse

3 **C'est un médecin**
  He's/She's a doctor
  Ce sont des acteurs
  They're actors

4 **Quelle surprise!**   **Quel idiot!**
  What a surprise!   What an idiot!

5 **avec une grande sagesse/un courage admirable**
  with great wisdom/admirable courage
  Il a fait preuve d'un sang-froid incroyable
  He showed incredible coolness
  Un film d'un mauvais goût désolant
  A film in appallingly bad taste

Adjectives

Most adjectives agree in number and in gender with the noun or pronoun.

The formation of feminines

- Most adjectives add an **e** to the masculine singular form (→**1**)
- If the masculine singular form already ends in **-e**, no further **e** is added (→**2**)
- Some adjectives undergo a further change when **e** is added. These changes occur regularly and are shown on p. 150
- Irregular feminine forms are shown on p. 152

The formation of plurals

- The plural of both regular and irregular adjectives is formed by adding an **s** to the masculine or feminine singular form, as appropriate (→**3**)
- When the masculine singular form already ends in **-s** or **-x**, no further **s** is added (→**4**)
- For masculine singulars ending in **-au** and **-eau**, the masculine plural is **-aux** and **-eaux** (→**5**)
- For masculine singulars ending in **-al**, the masculine plural is **-aux** (→**6**)

  Exceptions: **final** (masculine plural **finals**)
  fatal (masculine plural **fatals**)
  naval (masculine plural **navals**)

Pronunciation of feminine and plural adjectives

This is dealt with on p. 244

1 **mon frère aîné**   **ma sœur aînée**
    my elder brother   my elder sister
    le petit garçon   **la petite fille**
    the little boy   the little girl
    un sac gris   **une chemise grise**
    a grey bag   a grey shirt
    un bruit fort   **une voix forte**
    a loud noise   a loud voice

2 **un jeune homme**   **une jeune femme**
    a young man   a young woman
    l'autre verre   **l'autre assiette**
    the other glass   the other plate

3 **le dernier train**   **les derniers trains**
    the last train   the last trains
    une vieille maison   **de vieilles maisons**
    an old house   old houses
    un long voyage   **de longs voyages**
    a long journey   long journeys
    la rue étroite   **les rues étroites**
    the narrow street   the narrow streets

4 **un diplomate français**   **des diplomates français**
    a French diplomat   French diplomats
    un homme dangereux   **des hommes dangereux**
    a dangerous man   dangerous men

5 **le nouveau professeur**   **les nouveaux professeurs**
    the new teacher   the new teachers
    un chien esquimau   **des chiens esquimaux**
    a husky (Fr. = an Eskimo dog)   huskies (Fr. = Eskimo dogs)

6 **un ami loyal**   **des amis loyaux**
    a loyal friend   loyal friends
    un mari brutal   **des maris brutaux**
    a brutal husband   brutal husbands

Regular feminine endings

MASC. SING.	FEM. SING.	EXAMPLES	
-f	-ve	neuf, vif	(→1)
-x	-se	heureux, jaloux	(→2)
-eur	-euse	travailleur, flâneur	(→3)
-teur	-teuse	flatteur, menteur	(→4)
	-trice	destructeur, séducteur	(→5)

Exceptions:
   bref: see p. 152
   doux, faux, roux, vieux: see p. 152
   extérieur, inférieur, intérieur, meilleur, supérieur: all
   add **e** to the masculine
   enchanteur: fem. = **enchanteresse**

MASC. SING.	FEM. SING.	EXAMPLES	
-an	-anne	paysan	(→6)
-en	-enne	ancien, parisien	(→7)
-on	-onne	bon, breton	(→8)
-as	-asse	bas, las	(→9)
-et*	-ette	muet, violet	(→10)
-el	-elle	annuel, mortel	(→11)
-eil	-eille	pareil, vermeil	(→12)

Exception:
   ras: fem. = **rase**

MASC. SING.	FEM. SING.	EXAMPLES	
-et*	-ète	secret, complet	(→13)
-er	-ère	étranger, fier	(→14)

*Note that there are two feminine endings for masculine adjectives
ending in **-et**.

1 **un résultat positif**
   a positive result

   une attitude positive
   a positive attitude

2 **d'un ton sérieux**
   in a serious tone (of voice)

   une situation sérieuse
   a serious situation

3 **un enfant trompeur**
   a deceitful child

   une déclaration trompeuse
   a misleading statement

4 **un tableau flatteur**
   a flattering picture

   une comparaison flatteuse
   a flattering comparison

5 **un geste protecteur**
   a protective gesture

   une couche protectrice
   a protective layer

6 **un problème paysan**
   a farming problem

   la vie paysanne
   country life

7 **un avion égyptien**
   an Egyptian plane

   une statue égyptienne
   an Egyptian statue

8 **un bon repas**
   a good meal

   de bonne humeur
   in a good mood

9 **un plafond bas**
   a low ceiling

   à voix basse
   in a low voice

10 **un travail net**
   a clean piece of work

   une explication nette
   a clear explanation

11 **un homme cruel**
   a cruel man

   une remarque cruelle
   a cruel remark

12 **un livre pareil**
   such a book

   en pareille occasion
   on such an occasion

13 **un regard inquiet**
   an anxious look

   une attente inquiète
   an anxious wait

14 **un goût amer**
   a bitter taste

   une amère déception
   a bitter disappointment

Adjectives with irregular feminine forms

MASC. SING.	FEM. SING.		
aigu	aiguë	*sharp*	(→1)
ambigu	ambiguë	*ambiguous*	
beau (bel)★	belle	*beautiful*	
bénin	bénigne	*benign*	
blanc	blanche	*white*	
bref	brève	*brief, short*	(→2)
doux	douce	*soft; sweet*	
épais	épaisse	*thick*	
esquimau	esquimaude	*Eskimo*	
faux	fausse	*wrong*	
favori	favorite	*favourite*	(→3)
fou (fol)★	folle	*mad*	
frais	fraîche	*fresh*	(→4)
franc	franche	*frank*	
gentil	gentille	*kind*	
grec	grecque	*Greek*	
gros	grosse	*big*	
jumeau	jumelle	*twin*	(→5)
long	longue	*long*	
malin	maligne	*malignant*	
mou (mol)★	molle	*soft*	
nouveau (nouvel)★	nouvelle	*new*	
nul	nulle	*no*	
public	publique	*public*	(→6)
roux	rousse	*red-haired*	
sec	sèche	*dry*	
sot	sotte	*foolish*	
turc	turque	*Turkish*	
vieux (vieil)★	vieille	*old*	

★This form is used when the following word begins with a vowel o
an **h** 'mute' (→7)

1 **un bec aigu**
a sharp beak

une douleur aiguë
a sharp pain

2 **un bref discours**
a short speech

une brève rencontre
a short meeting

3 **mon sport favori**
my favourite sport

ma chanson favorite
my favourite song

4 **du pain frais**
fresh bread

de la crème fraîche
fresh cream

5 **mon frère jumeau**
my twin brother

ma sœur jumelle
my twin sister

6 **un jardin public**
a (public) park

l'opinion publique
public opinion

7 **un bel appartement**
a beautiful flat
le nouvel inspecteur
the new inspector
un vieil avare
an old miser

un bel habit
a beautiful outfit
un nouvel harmonica
a new harmonica
un vieil hôtel
an old hotel

154 ADJECTIVES

Comparatives and Superlatives

Comparatives
These are formed using the following constructions:

plus ... (que)	*more ... (than)*	(→1)
moins ... (que)	*less ... (than)*	(→2)
aussi ... que	*as ... as*	(→3)
si ... que*	*as ... as*	(→4)

*used mainly after a negative

Superlatives
These are formed using the following constructions:

le/la/les plus ... (que)	*the most ... (that)*	(→5)
le/la/les moins ... (que)	*the least ... (that)*	(→6)

- When the possessive adjective is present, two constructions are possible (→7)
- After a superlative the preposition **de** is often translated as *in* (→8)
- If a clause follows a superlative, the verb is in the subjunctive (→9)

Adjectives with irregular comparatives/superlatives

ADJECTIVE	COMPARATIVE	SUPERLATIVE
bon	**meilleur**	**le meilleur**
good	*better*	*the best*
mauvais	**pire** OR	**le pire** OR
bad	**plus mauvais**	**le plus mauvais**
	worse	*the worst*
petit	**moindre*** OR	**le moindre*** OR
small	**plus petit**	**le plus petit**
	smaller;	*the smallest;*
	lesser	*the least*

*used only with abstract nouns

- Comparative and superlative adjectives agree in number and in gender with the noun, just like any other adjective (→10)

1 **une raison plus grave**
   a more serious reason
   Elle est plus petite que ma sœur
   She is smaller than my sister

2 **un film moins connu**
   a less well-known film
   C'est moins cher qu'il ne pense
   It's cheaper than he thinks

3 **Paul était aussi inquiet que moi**
   Paul was as worried as I was
   Elle n'est pas aussi intelligente que ses parents
   She isn't as clever as her parents

4 **Ils ne sont pas si contents que ça**
   They aren't as happy as all that

5 **le guide le plus utile**   **l'auto la plus petite**
   the most useful guidebook   the smallest car
   les plus grandes maisons
   the biggest houses

6 **l'homme le moins agréable**   **la fille la moins forte**
   the least likeable man   the weakest girl
   les moins belles peintures
   the least attractive paintings

7 **Mon désir le plus cher** }
   Mon plus cher désir   } **est de voyager**
   My dearest wish is to travel

8 **la plus grande gare de Londres**
   the biggest station in London
   l'habitant le plus âgé du village/de la région
   the oldest inhabitant in the village/in the area

9 **la fille la plus gentille que je connaisse**
   the nicest girl I know

10 **les moindres difficultés**
   the least difficulties
   la meilleure qualité
   the best quality

Demonstrative Adjectives

	MASCULINE	FEMININE	
SING.	ce (cet)	cette	this; that
PLUR.	ces	ces	these; those

- Demonstrative adjectives agree in number and gender with the noun (→1)

- **cet** is used when the following word begins with a vowel or an **h** 'mute' (→2)

- For emphasis or in order to distinguish between people or objects, **-ci** or **-là** is added to the noun: **-ci** indicates proximity (usually translated *this*) and **-là** distance (*that*) (→3)

1 **Ce stylo ne marche pas**
   This/That pen isn't working
   Comment s'appelle cette fille?
   What's this/that girl called?
   Ces livres sont les miens
   These/Those books are mine
   Ces robes sont plus jolies
   These/Those dresses are nicer

2 **cet oiseau**
   this/that bird
   cet autre chapeau
   this/that other hat
   cet homme
   this/that man

3 **Combien coûte ce manteau-ci?**
   How much is this coat?
   Je voudrais cinq de ces pommes-là
   I'd like five of those apples
   Est-ce que tu reconnais ce monsieur-là?
   Do you recognise that gentleman?
   Mettez ces vêtements-ci dans cette valise-là
   Put these clothes in that case
   Ce garçon-là appartient à ce groupe-ci
   That boy belongs to this group

Interrogative Adjectives

	MASCULINE	FEMININE	
SING.	quel?	quelle?	*what?; which?*
PLUR.	quels?	quelles?	*what?; which?*

- Interrogative adjectives agree in number and gender with the noun (→**1**)

- The forms shown above are also used in indirect questions (→**2**)

Exclamatory Adjectives

	MASCULINE	FEMININE	
SING.	quel!	quelle!	*what (a)!*
PLUR.	quels!	quelles!	*what!*

- Exclamatory adjectives agree in number and gender with the noun (→**3**)

- For other exclamations, see p. 214

1 Quel genre d'homme est-ce?
What type of man is he?
Quelle est leur décision?
What is their decision?
Vous jouez de quels instruments?
What instruments do you play?
Quelles offres avez-vous reçues?
What offers have you received?
Quel vin recommandez-vous?
Which wine do you recommend?
Quelles filles sont les plus jeunes?
Which girls are the youngest?

2 Je ne sais pas à quelle heure il est arrivé
I don't know what time he arrived
Dites-moi quels sont les livres les plus intéressants
Tell me which books are the most interesting

3 Quel dommage!
What a pity!
Quelle loyauté!
What loyalty!
Quels beaux livres vous avez!
What fine books you have!
Quelles jolies fleurs!
What nice flowers!

Possessive Adjectives

WITH SING. NOUN		WITH PLUR. NOUN	
MASC.	FEM.	MASC./FEM.	
mon	ma (mon)	mes	*my*
ton	ta (ton)	tes	*your*
son	sa (son)	ses	*his; her; its*
notre	notre	nos	*our*
votre	votre	vos	*your*
leur	leur	leurs	*their*

- Possessive adjectives agree in number and gender with the noun, NOT WITH THE OWNER (→1)

- The forms shown in brackets are used when the following word begins with a vowel or an **h** 'mute'[1] (→2)

- **son, sa, ses** have the additional meaning of *one's* (→3)

1 **Martine a oublié son parapluie**
   Martine has left her umbrella
   Paul cherche sa montre
   Paul's looking for his watch
   Mon frère et ma sœur habitent à Paris
   My brother and sister live in Paris
   Est-ce que tes voisins ont vendu leur voiture?
   Did your neighbours sell their car?
   Rangez vos affaires
   Put your things away

2 **mon auto**
   my car
   ton haleine
   your breath
   son erreur
   his/her mistake
   mon autre sœur
   my other sister

3 **perdre son équilibre**
   to lose one's balance
   présenter ses excuses
   to offer one's apologies

Position of Adjectives

- French adjectives usually follow the noun (→**1**)

- Adjectives of colour or nationality *always* follow the noun (→**2**)

- As in English, demonstrative, possessive, numerical and interrogative adjectives precede the noun (→**3**)

- The adjectives **autre** *other* and **chaque** *each, every* precede the noun (→**4**)

- The following common adjectives can precede the noun:

beau	*beautiful*	**jeune**	*young*
bon	*good*	**joli**	*pretty*
court	*short*	**long**	*long*
dernier	*last*	**mauvais**	*bad*
grand	*great*	**petit**	*small*
gros	*big*	**tel**	*such (a)*
haut	*high*	**vieux**	*old*

- The meaning of the following adjectives varies according to their position:

	BEFORE NOUN	AFTER NOUN	
ancien	*former*	*old, ancient*	(→**5**)
brave	*good*	*brave*	(→**6**)
cher	*dear (beloved)*	*expensive*	(→**7**)
grand	*great*	*tall*	(→**8**)
même	*same*	*very*	(→**9**)
pauvre	*poor*	*poor*	
	(wretched)	*(not rich)*	(→**10**)
propre	*own*	*clean*	(→**11**)
seul	*single, sole*	*on one's own*	(→**12**)
simple	*mere, simple*	*simple, easy*	(→**13**)
vrai	*real*	*true*	(→**14**)

- Adjectives following the noun are linked by **et** (→**15**)

1 **le passage suivant**
   the following passage

   l'heure exacte
   the right time

2 **une cravate rouge**
   a red tie

   un mot français
   a French word

3 **ce chapeau**
   this hat

   mon père
   my father

   le premier étage
   the first floor

   deux exemples
   two examples

   quel homme?
   which man?

4 **une autre fois**
   another time

   chaque jour
   every day

5 **un ancien collègue**
   a former colleague

   l'histoire ancienne
   ancient history

6 **un brave homme**
   a good man

   un homme brave
   a brave man

7 **mes chers amis**
   my dear friends

   une robe chère
   an expensive dress

8 **un grand peintre**
   a great painter

   une dame grande
   a tall lady

9 **la même réponse**
   the same answer

   vos paroles mêmes
   your very words

10 **cette pauvre femme**
   that poor woman

   une nation pauvre
   a poor nation

11 **ma propre vie**
   my own life

   une chemise propre
   a clean shirt

12 **une seule réponse**
   a single reply

   une femme seule
   a woman on her own

13 **un simple regard**
   a mere look

   un problème simple
   a simple problem

14 **la vraie raison**
   the real reason

   les faits vrais
   the true facts

15 **un acte lâche et trompeur**
   a cowardly, deceitful act

   un acte lâche, trompeur et ignoble
   a cowardly, deceitful and ignoble act

Personal Pronouns

SUBJECT PRONOUNS

PERSON		SINGULAR	PLURAL
1st		**je (j')**	**nous**
		I	*we*
2nd		**tu**	**vous**
		you	*you*
3rd	(masc.)	**il**	**ils**
		he; it	*they*
	(fem.)	**elle**	**elles**
		she; it	*they*

je changes to **j'** before a vowel, an **h** 'mute', or the pronoun **y** (→1)

- **tu/vous**

  Vous, as well as being the second person plural, is also used when addressing one person. As a general rule, use **tu** only when addressing a friend, a child, a relative, someone you know very well, or when invited to do so. In all other cases use **vous**. For singular and plural uses of **vous**, see example 2.

- **il/elle; ils/elles**

  The form of the 3rd person pronouns reflects the number and gender of the noun(s) they replace, referring to animals and things as well as to people. **Ils** also replaces a combination of masculine and feminine nouns (→3)

- Sometimes stressed pronouns replace the subject pronouns, see p. 172

Continued

1 J'arrive!
I'm just coming!
J'en ai assez
I've enough
J'hésite à le déranger
I hesitate to disturb him
J'y pense souvent
I often think about it

2 Compare: **Vous êtes certain, Paul?**
Are you sure, Paul?
and: **Vous êtes certains, mes enfants?**
Are you sure, children?
Compare: **Vous êtes partie hier, Estelle?**
Did you leave yesterday, Estelle?
and: **Estelle et Sophie – vous êtes parties hier?**
Estelle and Sophie – did you leave yesterday?

3 Où logent ton père et ta mère quand ils vont à Rome?
Where do your father and mother stay when they go to Rome?
Donne-moi le journal et les lettres quand ils arriveront
Give me the newspaper and the letters when they arrive

Personal Pronouns (ctd.)

DIRECT OBJECT PRONOUNS

PERSON	SINGULAR	PLURAL
1st	**me (m')**	**nous**
	me	*us*
2nd	**te (t')**	**vous**
	you	*you*
3rd (masc.)	**le (l')**	**les**
	him; it	*them*
(fem.)	**la (l')**	**les**
	her; it	*them*

The forms shown in brackets are used before a vowel, an **h** 'mute', or the pronoun **y** (→**1**)

- In positive commands **me** and **te** change to **moi** and **toi** except before **en** or **y** (→**2**)

- **le** sometimes functions as a 'neuter' pronoun, referring to an idea or information contained in a previous statement or question. It is often not translated (→**3**)

Position of direct object pronouns
- In constructions other than the imperative affirmative the pronoun comes before the verb (→**4**)
  The same applies when the verb is in the infinitive (→**5**)
  In the imperative affirmative, the pronoun follows the verb and is attached to it by a hyphen (→**6**)

- For further information, see Order of Object Pronouns, p. 170

Reflexive Pronouns
These are dealt with under reflexive verbs, p. 30

Continued

1 **Il m'a vu**
He saw me
Je ne t'oublierai jamais
I'll never forget you
Ça l'habitue au froid
That gets him/her used to the cold
Je veux l'y accoutumer
I want to accustom him/her to it

2 **Avertis-moi de la décision** → **Avertis-m'en**
Inform me of the decision Inform me of it

3 **Il n'est pas là. – Je le sais bien.**
He isn't there. – I know that.
Aidez-moi si vous le pouvez
Help me if you can
Elle viendra demain. – Je l'espère bien.
She'll come tomorrow. – I hope so.

4 **Je t'aime**
I love you
Les voyez-vous?
Can you see them?
Elle ne nous connaît pas
She doesn't know us
Est-ce que tu ne les aimes pas?
Don't you like them?
Ne me quittez pas
Don't leave me

5 **Puis-je vous aider?**
May I help you?

6 **Aidez-moi** **Accompagnez-nous**
Help me Come with us

Personal Pronouns (ctd.)

INDIRECT OBJECT PRONOUNS

PERSON	SINGULAR	PLURAL
1st	me (m')	nous
2nd	te (t')	vous
3rd (masc.)	lui	leur
(fem.)	lui	leur

me and te change to m' and t' before a vowel or an h 'mute'
(→1)

- In positive commands, me and te change to moi and toi except before en (→2)

- The pronouns shown in the above table replace the preposition à + noun, where the noun is a person or an animal (→3)

- The verbal construction affects the translation of the pronoun (→4)

Position of indirect object pronouns
- In constructions other than the imperative affirmative, the pronoun comes before the verb (→5)
  The same applies when the verb is in the infinitive (→6)
  In the imperative affirmative, the pronoun follows the verb and is attached to it by a hyphen (→7)

- For further information, see Order of Object Pronouns, p. 170

Reflexive Pronouns
These are dealt with under reflexive verbs, p. 30

Continued

1 Tu m'as donné le livre
You gave me the book
Ils t'ont caché les faits
They hid the facts from you

2 **Donnez-moi du sucre**   → **Donnez-m'en**
Give me some sugar   Give me some
Garde-toi quelques livres → **Garde-t'en quelques-uns**
Keep some books for yourself Keep some for yourself

3 **J'écris à Suzanne**   → **Je lui écris**
I'm writing to Suzanne   I'm writing to her
Donne du lait au chat   → **Donne-lui du lait**
Give the cat some milk   Give it some milk

4 **arracher qch à qn**   to snatch sth from sb.
Un voleur m'a arraché mon porte-monnaie
A thief snatched my purse from me
promettre qch à qn   to promise sb sth:
Il leur a promis un cadeau
He promised them a present
demander à qn de faire   to ask sb to do:
Elle nous avait demandé de revenir
She had asked us to come back

5 **Elle vous a écrit**   **Vous a-t-elle écrit?**
She's written to you   Has she written to you?
Il ne nous parle pas
He doesn't speak to us
Est-ce qu'elle ne vous ressemble pas?
Doesn't she look like you?
Ne leur répondez pas
Don't answer them

6 **Voulez-vous leur envoyer l'adresse?**
Do you want to send them the address?

7 **Répondez-moi**   **Dites-nous la réponse**
Answer me   Tell us the answer

Personal Pronouns (ctd.)

Order of object pronouns

- When two object pronouns of different persons come before the verb, the order is: indirect before direct, i.e.

$$\left.\begin{array}{l} \textbf{me} \\ \textbf{te} \\ \textbf{nous} \\ \textbf{vous} \end{array}\right\} \text{ before } \left\{\begin{array}{l} \textbf{le} \\ \textbf{la} \\ \textbf{les} \end{array}\right. \quad (\rightarrow 1)$$

- When two 3rd person object pronouns come before the verb, the order is: direct before indirect, i.e.

$$\left.\begin{array}{l} \textbf{le} \\ \textbf{la} \\ \textbf{les} \end{array}\right\} \text{ before } \left\{\begin{array}{l} \textbf{lui} \\ \textbf{leur} \end{array}\right. \quad (\rightarrow 2)$$

- When two object pronouns come after the verb (i.e. in the imperative affirmative), the order is: direct before indirect, i.e.

$$\left.\begin{array}{l} \textbf{le} \\ \textbf{la} \\ \textbf{les} \end{array}\right\} \text{ before } \left\{\begin{array}{l} \textbf{moi} \\ \textbf{toi} \\ \textbf{lui} \\ \textbf{nous} \\ \textbf{vous} \\ \textbf{leur} \end{array}\right. \quad (\rightarrow 3)$$

- The pronouns **y** and **en** (see pp. 176 and 174) always come last (→4)

Continued

1 Martine vous l'envoie demain
Martine's sending it to you tomorrow
Est-ce qu'il te les a montrés?
Has he shown them to you?
Ne me le dis pas
Don't tell me (it)
Il ne veut pas nous la prêter
He won't lend it to us

2 Elle le leur a volé
She stole it from them
Je les lui ai lus
I read them to him/her
Ne la leur donne pas
Don't give it to them
Je voudrais les lui rendre
I'd like to give them back to him/her

3 Rends-les-moi
Give them back to me
Empruntez-le-nous
Borrow it from us
Apportons-les-leur
Let's take them to them

4 Donnez-leur-en
Give them some
Je l'y ai attaché
I tied it to it
Ne nous en parlez pas
Don't speak to us about it

Personal Pronouns (ctd.)

STRESSED OR DISJUNCTIVE PRONOUNS

PERSON	SINGULAR	PLURAL
1st	**moi**	**nous**
	me	*us*
2nd	**toi**	**vous**
	you	*you*
3rd (masc.)	**lui**	**eux**
	him; it	*them*
(fem.)	**elle**	**elles**
	her; it	*them*
('reflexive')	**soi**	
	oneself	

- These pronouns are used:
  - after prepositions (→**1**)
  - on their own (→**2**)
  - following **c'est, ce sont** *it is* (→**3**)
  - for emphasis, especially where contrast is involved (→**4**)
  - when the subject consists of two or more pronouns (→**5**)
  - when the subject consists of a pronoun and a noun (→**6**)
  - in comparisons (→**7**)
  - before relative pronouns (→**8**)

- For particular emphasis **-même** (singular) or **-mêmes** (plural) is added to the pronoun (→**9**):

moi-même	*myself*	**nous-mêmes**	*ourselves*
toi-même	*yourself*	**vous-même**	*yourself*
lui-même	*himself; itself*	**vous-mêmes**	*yourselves*
elle-même	*herself; itself*	**eux-mêmes**	*themselves*
soi-même	*oneself*	**elles-mêmes**	*themselves*

1 **Je pense à toi**
I think about you
C'est pour elle
This is for her
Venez avec moi
Come with me

Partez sans eux
Leave without them
Assieds-toi à côté de lui
Sit beside him
Il a besoin de nous
He needs us

2 **Qui l'a fait? – Lui.**
Who did it? – He did.
Qui est-ce qui gagne? – Moi
Who's winning? – Me

3 **C'est toi, Simon? – Non, c'est moi.**
Is that you, Simon? – No, it's me.
Qui est-ce? – Ce sont eux.
Who is it? – It's them.

4 **Ils voyagent séparément: lui par le train, elle en autobus**
They travel separately: he by train and she by bus
Toi, tu ressembles à ton père, eux pas
You look like your father, *they* don't
Il n'en sait rien, lui!
He knows nothing about it!

5 **Lui et moi partons demain**
He and I are leaving tomorrow
Ni vous ni elles ne restez
Neither you nor they are staying

6 **Mon père et elle ne s'entendent pas**
My father and she don't get on

7 **plus jeune que moi**
younger than me
Il est moins grand que toi
He's smaller than you (are)

8 **Moi, qui étais le cadet, j'ai dû rester à la maison**
I, who was the youngest, had to stay in the house
Ce sont eux qui font du bruit
They're the ones making the noise

9 **Je l'ai fait moi-même**
I did it myself

The pronoun en

- **en** replaces the preposition **de** + noun (→**1**)
  The verbal construction can affect the translation (→**2**)

- **en** also replaces the partitive article (*English = some, any*) + noun (→**3**)

- In expressions of quantity **en** represents the noun (→**4**)

- Position:
  en comes before the verb, except in positive commands when it follows and is attached to the verb by a hyphen (→**5**)

- **en** follows other object pronouns (→**6**)

1 **Il est fier de son succès** → **Il en est fier**
He's proud of his success   He's proud of it
Elle est sortie de la maison → **Elle en est sortie**
She came out of the house   She came out (of it)
Je suis couvert de boutons → **J'en suis couvert**
I'm covered in spots   I'm covered in them
Il a beaucoup d'amis → **Il en a beaucoup**
He has lots of friends   He has lots (of them)

2 **avoir besoin de qch**   to need sth:
J'en ai besoin
I need it/them

avoir peur de qch   to be afraid of sth:
J'en ai peur
I'm afraid of it/them

3 **Avez-vous de l'argent?** → **En avez-vous?**
Have you any money?   Do you have any?
Je veux acheter des bonbons → **Je veux en acheter**
I want to buy some sweets   I want to buy some

4 **J'ai deux crayons** → **J'en ai deux**
I've two pencils   I've two (of them)
Combien de sœurs as-tu? – **J'en ai trois.**
How many sisters do you have? – I have three.

5 **Elle en a discuté avec moi**
She discussed it with me
En êtes-vous content?
Are you pleased with it/them?
Je veux en garder trois
I want to keep three of them
N'en parlez plus
Don't talk about it any more
Prenez-en   **Soyez-en fier**
Take some   Be proud of it/them
6 **Donnez-leur-en**   **Il m'en a parlé**
Give them some   He spoke to me about it

The pronoun y

- y replaces the preposition **à** + noun (→**1**)
  The verbal construction can affect the translation (→**2**)

- y also replaces the prepositions **dans** and **sur** + noun (→**3**)

- y can also mean *there* (→**4**)

- Position:
  y comes before the verb, except in positive commands when it follows and is attached to the verb by a hyphen (→**5**)

- y follows other object pronouns (→**6**)

1 Ne touchez pas à ce bouton→ N'y touchez pas
Don't touch this switch   Don't touch it
Il participe aux concerts   → Il y participe
He takes part in the concerts He takes part (in them)

2 penser à qch to think about sth:
  J'y pense souvent
  I often think about it
  consentir à qch to agree to sth:
  Tu y as consenti?
  Have you agreed to it?

3 Mettez-les dans la boîte → Mettez-les-y
Put them in the box   Put them in it
Il les a mis sur les rayons → Il les y a mis
He put them on the shelves   He put them on them
Je compte sur votre aide   → J'y compte
I'm counting on your help   I'm counting on it

4 Elle y reste pendant l'été
She stays there during the summer

5 Il y a ajouté 50 francs
He added 50 francs to it
Elle n'y a pas écrit son nom
She hasn't written her name on it
Comment fait-on pour y aller?
How do you get there?
N'y pense plus!
Don't give it another thought!
Restez-y
Stay there
Réfléchissez-y
Think it over

6 Elle m'y a conduit
She drove me there
Menez-nous-y
Take us there

Indefinite Pronouns

aucun(e)	*none, not any*	(→1)
certain(e)s	*some, certain*	(→2)
chacun(e)	*each (one)*	(→3)
	everybody	
on	*one, you*	
	somebody	
	they, people	(→4)
	we (informal use)	
personne	*nobody*	(→5)
plusieurs	*several*	(→6)
quelque chose	*something; anything*	(→7)
quelques-un(e)s	*some, a few*	(→8)
quelqu'un	*somebody; anybody*	(→9)
rien	*nothing*	(→10)
tout	*all; everything*	(→11)
tous (toutes)	*all*	(→12)
l'un(e) ... l'autre	*(the) one ... the other*	
les un(e)s ... les autres	*some ... others*	(→13)

- **aucun(e), personne, rien**
  When used as subject or object of the verb, these require the word **ne** placed immediately before the verb. Note that **aucun** further needs the pronoun **en** when used as an object (→14)

- **quelque chose, rien**
  When qualified by an adjective, these pronouns require the preposition **de** before the adjective (→15)

1 Combien en avez-vous? – Aucun
How many have you got? – None

2 Certains pensent que ...
Some (people) think that ...

3 Chacune des boîtes est pleine   Chacun son tour!
Each of the boxes is full   Everybody in turn!

4 On voit l'église de cette fenêtre
You can see the church from this window
À la campagne on se couche tôt
In the country they/we go to bed early
Est-ce qu'on lui a permis de rester?
Was he/she allowed to stay?

5 Qui voyez-vous? – Personne
Who can you see? – Nobody

6 Plusieurs m'ont parlé
Several (people) spoke to me

7 Il mange quelque chose   Tu as vu quelque chose?
He's eating something   Did you see anything?

8 Je connais quelques-uns des noms
I know some of the names

9 Quelqu'un est tombé   Tu as vu quelqu'un?
Somebody has fallen   Did you see anybody?

10 Qu'est-ce que tu as dans la main? – Rien
What have you got in your hand? – Nothing

11 Il a tout gâché   Tout va bien
He has spoiled everything   All's well

12 Tu les as tous?   Elles sont toutes venues
Do you have all of them?   They all came

13 Les uns coûtent 20 francs, les autres 30 francs
Some cost 20 francs, (the) others 30 francs

14 Je ne vois personne   Rien ne lui plaît
I can't see anyone   Nothing pleases him/her
Aucune des filles ne veut ...   Il n'en a aucun
None of the girls wants ...   He hasn't any (of them)

15 quelque chose de grand   rien d'intéressant
something big   nothing interesting

Relative Pronouns

qui *who; which*
que *who(m); which*

These are subject and direct object pronouns that introduce a clause and refer to people or things.

		PEOPLE		THINGS	
SUBJECT		**qui**	(→1)	**qui**	(→3)
		who, that		*which, that*	
DIRECT OBJECT		**que (qu')**	(→2)	**que (qu')**	(→4)
		who(m), that		*which, that*	

- **que** changes to **qu'** before a vowel (→2/4)
- You cannot omit the object relative pronoun in French as you can in English (→2/4)

After a preposition:
- When referring to people, use **qui** (→5)
    Exceptions: after **parmi** *among* and **entre** *between* use **lesquels/lesquelles** (see below) (→6)
- When referring to things, use forms of **lequel**:

	MASCULINE	FEMININE	
SING.	**lequel**	**laquelle**	*which*
PLUR.	**lesquels**	**lesquelles**	*which*

The pronoun agrees in number and gender with the noun (→7)

- After the prepositions **à** and **de**, **lequel** and **lesquel(le)s** contract as follows:

    à + lequel → auquel
    à + lesquels → auxquels   (→8)
    à + lesquelles → auxquelles

    de + lequel → duquel
    de + lesquels → desquels   (→9)
    de + lesquelles → desquelles

Continued

1 **Mon frère, qui a vingt ans, est le cadet**
 My brother, who's twenty, is the youngest

2 **Les amis que j'aime le plus sont ...**
 The friends (that) I like best are ...
 Suzanne, qu'il admire, est ...
 Suzanne, whom he admires, is ...

3 **Il y a un escalier qui mène au toit**
 There's a staircase which leads to the roof

4 **La maison que nous avons achetée a ...**
 The house (which) we've bought has ...
 Voici le cadeau qu'elle m'a envoyé
 This is the present (that) she sent me

5 **la personne à qui il parle**
 the person he's talking to
 le garçon avec qui je joue
 the boy with whom I play
 les enfants pour qui je l'ai acheté
 the children for whom I bought it

6 **Il y avait des jeunes, parmi lesquels Paul**
 There were some young people, Paul among them
 les filles entre lesquelles j'étais assis
 the girls between whom I was sitting

7 **le torchon avec lequel il l'essuie**
 the cloth he's wiping it with
 la table sur laquelle je l'ai mis
 the table on which I put it
 les moyens par lesquels il l'accomplit
 the means by which he achieves it
 les pièces pour lesquelles elle est connue
 the plays for which she is famous

8 **le magasin auquel il livre ces marchandises**
 the shop to which he delivers these goods

9 **les injustices desquelles il se plaint**
 the injustices he's complaining about

Relative Pronouns (ctd.)

quoi *which, what*

- When the relative pronoun does not refer to a specific noun, **quoi** is used after a preposition (→1)

dont *whose, of whom, of which*

- **dont** often (but not always) replaces **de qui, duquel, de laquelle,** and **desquel(le)s** (→2)

- It cannot replace **de qui, duquel** etc in the construction preposition + noun + **de qui/duquel** (→3)

Continued

1 **C'est en quoi vous vous trompez**
That's where you're wrong
A quoi, j'ai répondu '...'
To which I replied, '...'

2 **la femme dont (=de qui) la fille est malade**
the woman whose daughter is ill
un fils dont (=de qui) je suis fier
a son I am proud of
un ami dont (=de qui) je connais le frère
a friend whose brother I know
les enfants dont (=de qui) vous vous occupez
the children you look after
le film dont (=duquel) il a parlé
the film of which he spoke
la fenêtre dont (=de laquelle) les rideaux sont tirés
the window whose curtains are drawn
des livres dont (=desquels) j'ai oublié les titres
books whose titles I've forgotten
les maladies dont (=desquelles) il souffre
the illnesses he suffers from

3 **une personne sur l'aide de qui on peut compter**
a person whose help one can rely on
les enfants aux parents de qui j'écris
the children to whose parents I'm writing
la maison dans le jardin de laquelle il y a ...
the house in whose garden there is ...

Relative Pronouns (ctd.)

ce qui, ce que *that which, what*
These are used when the relative pronoun does not refer to a specific noun, and they are often translated as *what* (literally: *that which*)

> **ce qui** is used as the subject (→1)
> **ce que*** is used as the direct object (→2)
>
> ***que** changes to **qu'** before a vowel (→2)

- Note the construction
  > **tout ce qui**
  > **tout ce que** } *everything/all that* (→3)

- **de + ce que → ce dont** (→4)

- **preposition + ce que → ce + preposition + quoi** (→5)

- When **ce qui, ce que** etc, refers to a previous CLAUSE the translation is *which* (→6)

1 Ce qui m'intéresse ne l'intéresse pas
What interests me doesn't interest him
Je n'ai pas vu ce qui s'est passé
I didn't see what happened

2 Ce que j'aime c'est la musique classique
What I like is classical music
Montrez-moi ce qu'il vous a donné
Show me what he gave you

3 Tout ce qui reste c'est ...
All that's left is ...
Donnez-moi tout ce que vous avez
Give me everything you have

4 Il risque de perdre ce dont il est si fier
He risks losing what he's so proud of
Voilà ce dont il s'agit
That's what it's about

5 Ce n'est pas ce à quoi je m'attendais
It's not what I was expecting
Ce à quoi je m'intéresse particulièrement c'est ...
What I'm particularly interested in is ...

6 Il est d'accord, ce qui m'étonne
He agrees, which surprises me
Il a dit qu'elle ne venait pas, ce que nous savions déjà
He said she wasn't coming, which we already knew

Interrogative Pronouns

qui? *who?; whom?*
que? *what?*
quoi? *what?*

These pronouns are used in direct questions.
The form of the pronoun depends on:
- whether it refers to people or to things
- whether it is the subject or object of the verb, or if it comes after a preposition

Qui and **que** have longer forms, as shown in the tables below.

- Referring to people:

SUBJECT	**qui?**	
	qui est-ce qui?	(→1)
	who?	
OBJECT	**qui?**	
	qui est-ce que*?	(→2)
	who(m)?	
AFTER PREPOSITIONS	**qui?**	(→3)
	who(m)?	

- Referring to things:

SUBJECT	**qu'est-ce qui?**	(→4)
	what?	
OBJECT	**que*?**	
	qu'est-ce que*?	(→5)
	what?	
AFTER PREPOSITIONS	**quoi?**	(→6)
	what?	

*que changes to **qu'** before a vowel (→2, 5)

Continued

1 **Qui vient?**
Qui est-ce qui vient?
Who's coming?

2 **Qui vois-tu?**
Qui est-ce que tu vois?
Who(m) can you see?
Qui a-t-elle rencontré?
Qui est-ce qu'elle a rencontré?
Who(m) did she meet?

3 **De qui parle-t-il?**
Who's he talking about?
Pour qui est ce livre?
Who's this book for?
A qui avez-vous écrit?
To whom did you write?

4 **Qu'est-ce qui se passe?**
What's happening?
Qu'est-ce qui a vexé Paul?
What upset Paul?

5 **Que faites-vous?**
Qu'est-ce que vous faites?
What are you doing?
Qu'a-t-il dit?
Qu'est-ce qu'il a dit?
What did he say?

6 **A quoi cela sert-il?**
What's that used for?
De quoi a-t-on parlé?
What was the discussion about?
Sur quoi vous basez-vous?
What do you base it on?

Interrogative Pronouns (ctd.)

qui *who; whom*
ce qui *what*
ce que *what*
quoi *what*

These pronouns are used in indirect questions.
The form of the pronoun depends on:
- whether it refers to people or to things
- whether it is the subject or object of the verb, or if it comes after a preposition

- Referring to people: use **qui** in all instances (→1)

- Referring to things:

SUBJECT	**ce qui**	(→2)
	what	
OBJECT	**ce que***	(→3)
	what	
AFTER PREPOSITIONS	**quoi**	(→4)
	what	

  ***que** changes to **qu'** before a vowel (→3)

Continued

1 **Demande-lui qui est venu**
   Ask him who came
   Je me demande qui ils ont vu
   I wonder who they saw
   Dites-moi qui vous aimez le plus
   Tell me who you like best
   Elle ne sait pas à qui s'adresser
   She doesn't know who to apply to
   Demandez-leur pour qui elles l'ont acheté
   Ask them who they bought it for

2 **Il demande ce qui se passe**
   He's asking what's happening
   Je ne sais pas ce qui vous fait croire que ...
   I don't know what makes you think that ...

3 **Raconte-nous ce que tu as fait**
   Tell us what you did
   Je me demande ce qu'elle pense
   I wonder what she's thinking

4 **On ne sait pas de quoi vivent ces animaux**
   We don't know what these animals live on
   Je vais lui demander à quoi il fait allusion
   I'm going to ask him what he's hinting at

Interrogative Pronouns (ctd.)

lequel?, laquelle?; lesquels?, lesquelles?

	MASCULINE	FEMININE	
SING.	**lequel?**	**laquelle?**	*which (one)?*
PLUR.	**lesquels?**	**lesquelles?**	*which (ones)?*

- The pronoun agrees in number and gender with the noun it refers to (→**1**)

- The same forms are used in indirect questions (→**2**)

- After the prepositions **à** and **de**, lequel and lesquel(le)s contract as follows:

  à + lequel? → auquel?
  à + lesquels? → auxquels?
  à + lesquelles? → auxquelles?

  de + lequel? → duquel?
  de + lesquels? → desquels?
  de + lesquelles? → desquelles?

1 **J'ai choisi un livre. – Lequel?**
  I've chosen a book. – Which one?
  Laquelle de ces valises est la vôtre?
  Which of these cases is yours?
  Amenez quelques amis. – Lesquels?
  Bring some friends. – Which ones?
  Lesquelles de vos sœurs sont mariées?
  Which of your sisters are married?

2 **Je me demande laquelle des chambres est la leur**
  I wonder which is their bedroom
  Dites-moi lesquels d'entre eux étaient là
  Tell me which of them were there

Possessive Pronouns

SINGULAR

MASCULINE	FEMININE	
le mien	la mienne	*mine*
le tien	la tienne	*yours*
le sien	la sienne	*his; hers; its*
le nôtre	la nôtre	*ours*
le vôtre	la vôtre	*yours*
le leur	la leur	*theirs*

PLURAL

MASCULINE	FEMININE	
les miens	les miennes	*mine*
les tiens	les tiennes	*yours*
les siens	les siennes	*his; hers; its*
les nôtres	les nôtres	*ours*
les vôtres	les vôtres	*yours*
les leurs	les leurs	*theirs*

- The pronoun agrees in number and gender with the noun it replaces, NOT WITH THE OWNER (→1)

- Alternative translations are *my own, your own* etc; **le sien, la sienne** etc. may also mean *one's own* (→2)

- After the prepositions **à** and **de** the articles **le** and **les** are contracted in the normal way (see p. 140):

  à + le mien → au mien
  à + les miens → aux miens   (→3)
  à + les miennes → aux miennes

  de + le mien → du mien
  de + les miens → des miens   (→4)
  de + les miennes → des miennes

1 **Demandez à Suzanne si ce stylo est le sien**
   Ask Suzanne if this pen is hers
   Quelle équipe a gagné – la leur ou la nôtre?
   Which team won – theirs or ours?
   Mon chien est plus jeune que le tien
   My dog is younger than yours
   Paul a pris mes affaires pour les siennes
   Paul mistook my belongings for his
   Si tu n'as pas de disques, emprunte les miens
   If you don't have any records, borrow mine
   Les pièces sont moins grandes que les vôtres
   The rooms are smaller than yours

2 **Est-ce que leur famille est aussi grande que la vôtre?**
   Is their family as big as your own?
   Leurs prix sont moins élevés que les nôtres
   Their prices are lower than our own
   Le bonheur des autres importe plus que le sien
   Other people's happiness matters more than one's own

3 **Pourquoi préfères-tu ce chapeau au mien?**
   Why do you prefer this hat to mine?
   Quelles maisons ressemblent aux leurs?
   Which houses resemble theirs?

4 **Leur père habite près du vôtre**
   Their father lives near yours
   Vos livres sont au-dessus des miens
   Your books are on top of mine

Demonstrative Pronouns

celui, celle; ceux, celles

	MASCULINE	FEMININE	
SING.	**celui**	**celle**	*the one*
PLUR.	**ceux**	**celles**	*the ones*

- The pronoun agrees in number and gender with the noun it replaces (→**1**)

- Uses:
  - preceding a relative pronoun, meaning *the one(s) who/which* (→**1**)
  - preceding the preposition **de**, meaning *the one(s) belonging to, the one(s) of* (→**2**)
  - with **-ci** and **-là**, for emphasis or to distinguish between two things:

	MASCULINE	FEMININE		
SING.	**celui-ci**	**celle-ci**	*this (one)*	(→**3**)
PLUR.	**ceux-ci**	**celles-ci**	*these (ones)*	

	MASCULINE	FEMININE		
SING.	**celui-là**	**celle-là**	*that (one)*	(→**3**)
PLUR.	**ceux-là**	**celles-là**	*those (ones)*	

  - an additional meaning of **celui-ci/celui-là** etc. is *the former/the latter*

Continued

1 **Lequel? – Celui qui parle à Suzanne**
    Which man? – The one who's talking to Suzanne
    Quelle robe désirez-vous? – Celle qui est en vitrine
    Which dress do you want? – The one which is in the window
    Est-ce que ces livres sont ceux qu'il t'a donnés?
    Are these the books that he gave you?
    Quelles filles? – Celles que nous avons vues hier
    Which girls? – The ones we saw yesterday
    Cet article n'est pas celui dont vous m'avez parlé
    This article isn't the one you spoke to me about

2 **Le jardin est plus grand que celui de mes parents**
    The garden is bigger than my parents' (garden)
    Est-ce que ta fille est plus âgée que celle de Sophie?
    Is your daughter older than Sophie's (daughter)?
    Je préfère les enfants de Paul à ceux de Roger
    I prefer Paul's children to Roger's (children)
    Comparez vos réponses à celles de votre voisin
    Compare your answers with your neighbour's (answers)
    les montagnes d'Ecosse et celles du pays de Galles
    the mountains of Scotland and those of Wales

3 **Quel tailleur préférez-vous: celui-ci ou celui-là?**
    Which suit do you prefer: this one or that one?
    Cette chemise coûte 100 francs et celle-là 150 francs
    This shirt costs 100 francs and that one 150 francs
    Quels œufs devrais-je acheter: ceux-ci ou ceux-là?
    Which eggs should I buy: these (ones) or those (ones)?
    De toutes mes jupes, celle-ci me va le mieux
    Of all my skirts, this one fits me best

Demonstrative Pronouns (ctd.)

ce (c') *it, that*

- Usually used with **être**, in the expressions **c'est, c'était, ce sont** etc. (→**1**)

- Note the spelling **ç** when followed by the letter **a** (→**2**)

- Uses:
  - to identify a person or object (→**3**)
  - for emphasis (→**4**)
  - as a neuter pronoun, referring to a statement, idea etc. (→**5**)

ce qui, ce que, ce dont etc.: see Relative Pronouns (p. 184), Interrogative Pronouns (p. 188)

cela, ça *it, that*

- **cela** and **ça** are used as 'neuter' pronouns, referring to a statement, an idea, an object (→**6**)

- In everyday spoken language **ça** is used in preference to **cela**

ceci *this* (→**7**)

- **ceci** is not used as often as 'this' in English; **cela, ça** are often used where we use 'this'

1 **C'est ...**
It's/That's ...

C'était moi
It was me

2 **Ça a été la cause de ...**
It has been the cause of ...

3 **Qui est-ce?**
Who is it?; Who's this/that?; Who's he/she?

C'est lui/mon frère/nous
It's/That's him/my brother/us

Ce sont eux
It's them

C'est une infirmière
She's a nurse

Ce sont des professeurs
They're teachers

Qu'est-ce que c'est?
What's this/that?

Qu'est-ce que c'est que ça?
What's that?

C'est un coupe-papier
It's a paper knife

Ce sont des pinces à épiler
They're tweezers

4 **C'est moi qui ai téléphoné**
It was me who phoned

Ce sont les enfants qui importent le plus
It's the children who matter most

5 **C'est bien intéressant**
That's/It's very interesting

Ce serait dangereux
That/It would be dangerous

6 **Ça ne fait rien**
It doesn't matter

A quoi bon faire ça?
What's the use of doing that?

Cela ne compte pas
That doesn't count

Cela demande du temps
It/That takes time

7 **A qui est ceci?**
Whose is this?

Tenez-le comme ceci
Hold it like this

Adverbs

Formation

- Most adverbs are formed by adding **-ment** to the feminine form of the adjective (→1)

- **-ment** is added to the *masculine* form when the masculine form ends in **-é**, **-i** or **-u** (→2)
  Exception: **gai** (→3)
  Occasionally the **u** changes to **û** before **-ment** is added (→4)

- If the adjective ends in **-ant** or **-ent**, the adverb ends in **-amment** or **-emment** (→5)
  Exceptions: **lent**, **présent** (→6)

Irregular Adverbs

ADJECTIVE		ADVERB		
aveugle	blind	aveuglément	blindly	
bon	good	bien	well	(→7)
bref	brief	brièvement	briefly	
énorme	enormous	énormément	enormously	
exprès	express	expressément	expressly	(→8)
gentil	kind	gentiment	kindly	
mauvais	bad	mal	badly	(→9)
meilleur	better	mieux	better	
pire	worse	pis	worse	
précis	precise	précisément	precisely	
profond	deep	profondément	deeply	(→10)
traître	treacherous	traîtreusement	treacherously	

Adjectives used as adverbs

Certain adjectives are used adverbially. These include: **bas, bon, cher, clair, court, doux, droit, dur, faux, ferme, fort, haut, mauvais** and **net** (→11)

1 MASC./FEM. ADJECTIVE   ADVERB
   heureux/heureuse fortunate   **heureusement** fortunately
   franc/franche frank   **franchement** frankly
   extrême/extrême extreme   **extrêmement** extremely
2 MASC. ADJECTIVE   ADVERB
   désespéré desperate   **désespérément** desperately
   vrai true   **vraiment** truly
   résolu resolute   **résolument** resolutely
3 **gai** gay   **gaiement** OR **gaîment** gaily
4 **continu** continous   **continûment** continuously
5 **constant** constant   **constamment** constantly
   courant fluent   **couramment** fluently
   évident obvious   **évidemment** obviously
   fréquent frequent   **fréquemment** frequently
6 **lent** slow   **lentement** slowly
   présent present   **présentement** presently
7 **Elle travaille bien**
   She works well
8 **Il a expressément défendu qu'on parte**
   He has expressly forbidden us to leave
9 **Un emploi mal payé**
   A badly paid job
0 **J'ai été profondément ému**
   I was deeply moved
1 **parler bas/haut**
   to speak softly/loudly
   coûter cher
   to be expensive
   voir clair
   to see clearly
   travailler dur
   to work hard
   chanter faux
   to sing off key
   sentir bon/mauvais
   to smell nice/horrible

Position of Adverbs

- When the adverb accompanies a verb in a simple tense, it generally follows the verb (→1)
- When the adverb accompanies a verb in a compound tense, it generally comes between the auxiliary verb and the past participle (→2)
  Some adverbs, however, follow the past participle (→3)
- When the adverb accompanies an adjective or another adverb it generally precedes the adjective/adverb (→4)

Comparatives of Adverbs

These are formed using the following constructions:

plus ... (que)   *more ... (than)* (→5)
moins ... (que)   *less ... (than)* (→6)
aussi ... que   *as ... as*   (→7)
si ... que*   *as ... as*   (→8)
*used mainly after a negative

Superlatives of Adverbs

These are formed using the following constructions:

le plus ... (que)   *the most ... (that)* (→9)
le moins ... (que)   *the least ... (that)* (→10)

Adverbs with irregular comparatives/superlatives

ADVERB	COMPARATIVE	SUPERLATIVE
beaucoup	**plus**	**le plus**
a lot	*more*	*(the) most*
bien	**mieux**	**le mieux**
well	*better*	*(the) best*
mal	**pis** OR	**le pis** OR
	plus mal	**le plus mal**
badly	*worse*	*(the) worst*
peu	**moins**	**le moins**
little	*less*	*(the) least*

1   **Il dort encore**   **Je pense souvent à toi**
    He's still asleep   I often think about you

2   **Ils sont déjà partis**   **J'ai toujours cru que ...**
    They've already gone   I've always thought that ...
    J'ai presque fini   **Il a trop mangé**
    I'm almost finished   He's eaten too much

3   **On les a vus partout**   **Elle est revenue hier**
    We saw them everywhere   She came back yesterday

4   **un très beau chapeau**   **une dame bien habillée**
    a very nice hat   a well-dressed lady
    beaucoup plus vite   **peu souvent**
    much faster   not very often

5   **plus vite**   **plus régulièrement**
    more quickly   more regularly
    Elle chante plus fort que moi
    She sings louder than I do

6   **moins facilement**   **moins souvent**
    less easily   less often
    Nous nous voyons moins fréquemment qu'auparavant
    We see each other less frequently than before

7   **Faites-le aussi vite que possible**
    Do it as quickly as possible
    Ils gagnent aussi peu que nous
    They earn as little as we do

8   **Ce n'est pas si loin que je pensais**
    It's not as far as I thought

9   **Gabrielle court le plus vite**
    Gabrielle runs fastest
    Le plus tôt que je puisse venir c'est samedi
    The earliest that I can come is Saturday

10 **Lesquels de tes amis vois-tu le moins souvent?**
    Which of your friends do you see least often?

Common adverbs and their usage

assez	*enough; quite*	(→1) See also below
aussi	*also, too; as*	(→2)
autant	*as much*	(→3) See also below
beaucoup	*a lot; much*	(→4) See also below
bien	*well; very*	(→5) See also below
	very much; 'indeed'	
combien	*how much; how many*	(→6) See also below
comme	*how; what*	(→7)
déjà	*already; before*	(→8)
encore	*still; yet*	(→9)
	more; even	
moins	*less*	(→10) See also below
peu	*little, not much; not very*	(→11) See also below
plus	*more*	(→12) See also below
si	*so; such*	(→13)
tant	*so much*	(→14) See also below
toujours	*always; still*	(→15)
trop	*too much; too*	(→16) See also below

- **assez, autant, beaucoup, combien** etc. are used in the construction *adverb + de + noun* with the following meanings:

assez de	*enough*
autant de	*as much; as many*
	so much; so many
beaucoup de	*a lot of*
combien de	*how much; how many* (→17)
moins de	*less; fewer*
peu de	*little, not much; few,*
	not many
plus de	*more*
tant de	*so much; so many*
trop de	*too much; too many*

- **bien** can be followed by a partitive article (see p. 144) plus a noun to mean *a lot of; a good many* (→18)

1 **Avez-vous assez chaud?**   **Il est assez tard**
Are you warm enough?   It's quite late

2 **Je l'aime aussi**   **Elle est aussi grande que moi**
I like it too   She is as tall as I am

3 **Je gagne autant que Simon**   I earn as much as Simon

4 **Tu lis beaucoup?**   **C'est beaucoup plus loin?**
Do you read a lot?   Is it much further?

5 **Bien joué!**   **Je suis bien content que …**
Well played!   I'm very pleased that …
Il s'est bien amusé   **Je l'ai bien fait**
He enjoyed himself very much   I DID do it

6 **Combien coûte ce livre?**   **Vous êtes combien?**
How much is this book?   How many of you are there?

7 **Comme tu es jolie!**   **Comme il fait beau!**
How pretty you look!   What lovely weather!

8 **Je l'ai déjà fait**   **Êtes-vous déjà allé en France?**
I've already done it   Have you been to France before?

9 **J'en ai encore deux**   **Elle n'est pas encore là**
I've still got two   She isn't there yet
Encore du café, Paul?   **Encore mieux!**
More coffee, Paul?   Even better!

10 **Mangez moins**   **Je suis moins étonné que toi**
Eat less   I'm less surprised than you are

11 **Elle mange peu**   **C'est peu important**
She doesn't eat very much   It's not very important

12 **Il travaille plus**   **Elle est plus timide que Sophie**
He works more   She is shyer than Sophie

13 **Roger est si charmant**   **une si belle vue**
Roger is so charming   such a lovely view

14 **Elle l'aime tant** She loves him so much

15 **Il dit toujours ça!**   **Tu le vois toujours?**
He always says that!   Do you still see him?

16 **J'ai trop mangé**   **C'est trop cher**
I've eaten too much   It's too expensive

17 **assez d'argent/de livres**   **moins de temps/d'amis**
enough money/books   less time/fewer friends

18 **bien du mal/des gens** a lot of harm/a good many people

On the following pages you will find some of the most frequent uses of prepositions in French. Particular attention is paid to cases where usage differs markedly from English. It is often difficult to give an English equivalent for French prepositions, since usage *does* vary so much between the two languages.

In the list below, the broad meaning of the preposition is given on the left, with examples of usage following.

Prepositions are dealt with in alphabetical order, except **à**, **de** and **en** which are shown first.

à

at	**lancer qch à qn**	*to throw sth at sb*
	il habite à St. Pierre	*he lives at St. Pierre*
	à 5 francs la pièce	*(at) 5 francs each*
	à 100 km à l'heure	*at 100 km per hour*
in	**à la campagne**	*in the country*
	à Londres	*in London*
	au lit	*in bed (also to bed)*
	un livre à la main	*with a book in his/her hand*
on	**un tableau au mur**	*a picture on the wall*
to	**aller au cinéma**	*to go to the cinema*
	donner qch à qn	*to give sth to sb*
	le premier/dernier à faire	*the first/last to do*
	demander qch à qn	*to ask sb sth*
from	**arracher qch à qn**	*to snatch sth from sb*
	acheter qch à qn	*to buy sth from sb*
	cacher qch à qn	*to hide sth from sb*
	emprunter qch à qn	*to borrow sth from sb*
	prendre qch à qn	*to take sth from sb*
	voler qch à qn	*to steal sth from sb*

descriptive	**la femme au chapeau vert**	*the woman with the green hat*
	un garçon aux cheveux mal peignés	*a boy with untidy hair*
manner, means	**à l'anglaise**	*in the English manner*
	à la main	*by hand*
	à bicyclette/cheval	*by bicycle/on horseback* (BUT note other forms of transport used with en and par)
	à pied	*on foot*
	chauffer au gaz	*to heat with/by gas*
	à pas lents	*with slow steps*
	verni à la laque	*varnished with lacquer*
time, date: *at, in*	**à minuit**	*at midnight*
	à trois heures cinq	*at five past three*
	au 20ème siècle	*in the 20th century*
	à Noël/Pâques	*at Christmas/Easter*
distance	**à 6 km d'ici**	*(at a distance of) 6 km from here*
	à deux pas de chez moi	*just a step from my place*
destined for	**une tasse à thé**	*a teacup* (compare **une tasse de thé**)
	un service à café	*a coffee service*
after certain adjectives	**son écriture est difficile à lire**	*his writing is difficult to read* (compare the usage with de, p. 206)
	prêt à tout	*ready for anything*
after certain verbs *Continued*	see p. 64	

de

from	**venir de Londres**	*to come from London*
	du matin au soir	*from morning till night*
	du 21 juin au 5 juillet	*from 21st June till 5th July*
	de 10 à 15	*from 10 to 15*
belonging to, *of*	**le chapeau de mon père**	*my father's hat*
	les vents d'automne	*the autumn winds*
contents, composition, material	**une boîte d'allumettes**	*a box of matches*
	une tasse de thé	*a cup of tea (compare* **une tasse à thé***)*
	une robe de soie	*a silk dress*
manner	**d'une façon irrégulière**	*in an irregular way*
	d'un coup de couteau	*with the blow of a knife*
quality	**un homme de raison**	*a man of reason*
	des objets de valeur	*valuable items*
comparative + a number	**il y avait plus/moins de cent personnes**	*there were more/fewer than a hundred people*
after superlatives: *in*	**la plus/moins belle ville du monde**	*the most/least beautiful city in the world*
after certain adjectives	**content de voir**	*pleased to see*
	il est difficile d'y accéder	*access is difficult (compare the usage with* **à***, p. 205)*
after certain verbs	see p. 64	

en

place: *to, in, on*	**en ville**	*in/to town*
	en pleine mer	*on the open sea*
	en France	*in/to France* (note that masculine countries use **à**)
dates, months: *in*	**en 1923**	*in 1923*
	en janvier	*in January*
transport	**en auto/voiture**	*by car*
	en avion	*by plane* (but note usage of **à** and **par** in other expressions)
language	**en français**	*in French*
duration	**je le ferai en huit jours**	*I'll do it in eight days* (i.e. *I'll take 8 days to do it*: compare **dans huit jours**)
material	**un bracelet en or**	*a bracelet made of gold* (note that the use of **en** stresses the material more than the use of **de**)
	consister en	*to consist of*
in the manner of, like a	**parler en vrai homme du monde**	*to speak like a real man of the world*
	déguisé en cowboy	*dressed up as a cowboy*
+ present participle	**il l'a vu en passant devant la porte**	*he saw it as he came past the door*

Continued

avant

before	**il est arrivé avant toi**	*he arrived before you*
+ infinitive (add **de**)	**je vais finir ça avant de manger**	*I'm going to finish this before eating*
preference	**la santé avant tout**	*health above all things*

chez

at the home of	**chez lui/moi** **être chez soi** **venez chez nous**	*at his/my house* *to be at home* *come round to our place*
at/to a shop	**chez le boucher**	*at/to the butcher's*
in a person, *among* a group of people	**ce que je n'aime pas chez lui c'est son ...** **chez les politiciens**	*what I don't like in him is his ...* *among politicians*

dans

position	**dans une boîte**	*in(to) a box*
circumstance	**dans son enfance**	*in his childhood*
future time	**dans huit jours**	*in eight days' time* (compare **en huit jours**, p. 207)

depuis

since: time	**depuis mardi**	*since Tuesday*
place	**il pleut depuis Paris**	*it's been raining since Paris*
for	**il habite cette maison depuis 3 ans**	*he's been living in this house for 3 years* (NOTE TENSE)

dès

past time	**dès mon enfance**	*since my childhood*
future time	**je le ferai dès mon retour**	*I'll do it as soon as I get back*

entre

between	**entre 8 et 10**	*between 8 and 10*
among	**Jean et Pierre, entre autres**	*Jean and Pierre, among others*
reciprocal	**s'aider entre eux**	*to help each other (out)*

d'entre

of, among	**trois d'entre eux**	*three of them*

par

agent of passive: by	**renversé par une voiture**	*knocked down by a car*
	tué par la foudre	*killed by lightning*
weather conditions	**par un beau jour d'été**	*on a lovely summer's day*
by (means of)	**par un couloir/sentier**	*by a corridor/path*
	par le train	*by train (but see also à and en)*
	par l'intermédiaire de M. Leblanc	*through Mr. Leblanc*
distribution	**deux par deux**	*two by two*
	par groupes de dix	*in groups of ten*
	deux fois par jour	*twice a day*

continued

pour

for		
	c'est pour vous	it's for you
	c'est pour demain	it's for tomorrow
	une chambre pour 2 nuits	a room for 2 nights
	pour un enfant, il est très doué	for a child he's very good (at it)
	il part pour l'Espagne	he's leaving for Spain
	il l'a fait pour vous	he did it for you
	il lui a donné 50 francs pour ce livre	he gave him 50 francs for this book
	je ne suis pas pour cette idée	I'm not for that idea
	pour qui me prends-tu?	who do you take me for?
	il passe pour un idiot	he's taken for a fool
+ infinitive: (in order) to	elle se pencha pour le ramasser	she bent down to pick it up
	il est trop bête pour comprendre	he's too stupid to understand
to(wards)	être bon/gentil pour qn	to be kind to sb
with prices, time	pour 100 francs d'essence	100 francs' worth of petrol
	j'en ai encore pour une heure	I'll be another hour (at it) yet

sans

without		
	sans eau	without water
	sans ma femme	without my wife
+ infinitive	sans compter les autres	without counting the others

sauf

xcept (for)	**tous sauf lui**	*all except him*
	sauf quand il pleut	*except when it's raining*
arring	**sauf imprévu**	*barring the unexpected*
	sauf avis contraire	*unless you hear to the contrary*

sur

n	**sur le siège**	*on the seat*
	sur l'armoire	*on top of the wardrobe*
	sur le mur	*on (top of) the wall (if the meaning is hanging on the wall use à, p. 204)*
	sur votre gauche	*on your left*
	être sur le point de faire	*to be on the point of doing*
x (to)	**mettez-le sur la table**	*put it on the table*
roportion: t of; by	**8 sur 10**	*8 out of 10*
	un automobiliste sur 5	*one motorist in 5*
	la pièce fait 2 mètres sur 3	*the room measures 2 metres by 3*

Conjunctions

There are conjunctions which introduce a main clause, such as **et** *and*, **mais** *but*, **si** *if*, **ou** *or* etc., and those which introduce subordinate clauses like **parce que** *because*, **pendant que** *while*, **après que** *after* etc. They are all used in much the same way as in English, but the following points are of note:

- Some conjunctions in French require a following subjunctive, see p. 58

- Some conjunctions are 'split' in French like *both ... and*, *either ... or* in English:

et ... et	*both ... and*	(→1)
ni ... ni ... ne	*neither ... nor*	(→2)
ou (bien) ... ou (bien)	*either ... or (else)*	(→3)
soit ... soit	*either ... or*	(→4)

- **si + il(s) → s'il(s)** (→5)

- **que**
  - meaning *that* (→6)
  - replacing another conjunction (→7)
  - replacing **si**, see p. 62
  - in comparisons, meaning *as*, *than* (→8)
  - followed by the subjunctive, see p. 62

- **aussi** *so*, *therefore*: the subject and verb are inverted if the subject is a pronoun (→9)

1 Ces fleurs poussent et en été et en hiver
These flowers grow in both summer and winter

2 Ni lui ni elle ne sont venus
Neither he nor she came
Je n'ai ni argent ni nourriture
I have neither money nor food

3 Elle doit être ou naïve ou stupide
She must be either naïve or stupid
Ou bien il m'évite ou bien il ne me reconnaît pas
Either he's avoiding me or else he doesn't recognise me

4 Il faut choisir soit l'un soit l'autre
You have to choose either one or the other

5 Je ne sais pas s'il vient/s'ils viennent
I don't know if he's coming/if they're coming
Dis-moi s'il y a des erreurs
Tell me if there are any mistakes
Votre passeport, s'il vous plaît
Your passport, please

6 Il dit qu'il t'a vu
He says (that) he saw you
Est-ce qu'elle sait que vous êtes là?
Does she know that you're here?

7 Quand tu seras plus grand et que tu auras une maison à toi, ...
When you're older and you have a house of your own, ...
Comme il pleuvait et que je n'avais pas de parapluie, ...
As it was raining and I didn't have an umbrella, ...

8 Ils n'y vont pas aussi souvent que nous
They don't go there as often as we do
Il les aime plus que jamais
He likes them more than ever
Elle est moins belle que sa sœur
She's less attractive than her sister

9 Ceux-ci sont plus rares, aussi coûtent-ils cher
These ones are rarer, so they're expensive

Word Order

Word order in French is largely the same as in English, except for the following. Most of these have already been dealt with under the appropriate part of speech, but are summarised here along with other instances not covered elsewhere.

- Object pronouns nearly always come before the verb (→**1**)
  For details, see pp. 166 to 170

- Certain adjectives come after the noun (→**2**)
  For details, see p. 162

- Adverbs accompanying a verb in a simple tense usually follow the verb (→**3**)
  For details, see p. 200

- After **aussi** *so, therefore*, **à peine** *hardly*, **peut-être** *perhaps*, the verb and subject are inverted (→**4**)

- After the relative pronoun **dont** *whose* (→**5**)
  For details, see p. 182

- In exclamations, **que** and **comme** do not affect the normal word order (→**6**)

- Following direct speech:
  - the *verb* + *subject* order is inverted to become *subject* + *verb* (→**7**)
  - with a pronoun subject, the verb and pronoun are linked by a hyphen (→**8**)
  - when the verb ends in a vowel in the 3rd person singular, **-t-** is inserted between the pronoun and the verb (→**9**)

For word order in negative sentences, see p. 216
For word order in interrogative sentences, see pp. 220 and 222

1 **Je les vois!**
  I can see them!

  Il me l'a donné
  He gave it to me

2 **une ville française**
  a French town

  du vin rouge
  some red wine

3 **Il pleut encore**
  It's still raining

  Elle m'aide quelquefois
  She sometimes helps me

4 **Il vit tout seul, aussi fait-il ce qu'il veut**
  He lives alone, so he does what he likes

  A peine la pendule avait-elle sonné trois heures que ...
  Hardly had the clock struck three when ...

  Peut-être avez-vous raison
  Perhaps you're right

5 Compare: **un homme dont je connais la fille**
              a man whose daughter I know

  and: **un homme dont la fille me connaît**
              a man whose daughter knows me

  If the person (or object) 'owned' is the *object* of the verb, the order is:
  dont + verb + noun (1st sentence)
  If the person (or object) 'owned' is the *subject* of the verb, the order is:
  dont + noun + verb (2nd sentence)

  Note also: **l'homme dont elle est la fille**
                the man whose daughter she is

6 **Qu'il fait chaud!**
  How warm it is!

  Que je suis content de vous voir!
  How pleased I am to see you!

  Comme c'est cher!
  How expensive it is!

  Que tes voisins sont gentils!
  How kind your neighbours are!

7 **'Je pense que oui' a dit Marie**
  'I think so,' said Marie

  'Ça ne fait rien' répondit Martin
  'It doesn't matter,' Martin replied

8 **'Quelle horreur!' me suis-je exclamé**
  'How awful!' I exclaimed

9 **'Pourquoi pas?' a-t-elle demandé**
  'Why not?' she asked

  'Si c'est vrai,' continua-t-il ' ... '
  'If it's true,' he went on ' ... '

Negatives

ne ... pas	*not*
ne ... point (literary)	*not*
ne ... rien	*nothing*
ne ... personne	*nobody*
ne ... plus	*no longer*
ne ... jamais	*never*
ne ... que	*only*
ne ... aucun(e)	*no*
ne ... nul(le)	*no*
ne ... nulle part	*nowhere*
ne ... ni	*neither ... nor*
ne ... ni ... ni	*neither ... nor*

● **Word order**

– In simple tenses and the imperative:
  ne precedes the verb (and any object pronouns) and the second
  element follows the verb (→**1**)

– In compound tenses:
  i ne ... pas, ne ... point, ne ... rien, ne ... plus, ne ..
    jamais, ne ... guère follow the pattern:
    ne + auxiliary verb + **pas** + past participle (→**2**)
  ii ne ... personne, ne ... que, ne ... aucun(e), ne ... nul(le)
    ne ... nulle part, ne ... ni (... ni) follow the pattern:
    ne + auxiliary verb + past participle + **personne** (→**3**)

– With a verb in the infinitive:
  ne ... pas, **ne ... point** (etc. see i above) come together (→**4**

● For use of **rien**, **personne** and **aucun** as pronouns, see p. 17

Continued

1 **Je ne fume pas**
I don't smoke
Ne changez rien
Don't change anything
Je ne vois personne
I can't see anybody
Nous ne nous verrons plus
We won't see each other any more
Je ne vous oublierai jamais
I'll never forget you
Il n'avait que dix francs
He only had ten francs
Je n'ai aucune idée
I've no idea
Il ne boit ni ne fume
He neither drinks nor smokes
Ni mon fils ni ma fille ne les connaissaient
Neither my son nor my daughter knew them

2 **Elle n'a pas fait ses devoirs**
She hasn't done her homework
Ne vous a-t-il rien dit?
Didn't he say anything to you?
Ils n'avaient jamais vu une si belle maison
They had never seen such a beautiful house
Tu n'as guère changé
You've hardly changed

3 **Je n'ai parlé à personne**
I haven't spoken to anybody
Il n'avait mangé que la moitié du repas
He had only eaten half the meal
Elle ne les a trouvés nulle part
She couldn't find them anywhere
Il ne l'avait ni vu ni entendu
He had neither seen nor heard him

4 **Il essayait de ne pas rire**
He was trying not to laugh

Negatives (ctd.)

- Combination of negatives.
  These are the most common combinations of negative particles:

ne ... plus jamais	(→1)
ne ... plus personne	(→2)
ne ... plus rien	(→3)
ne ... plus ni ... ni ...	(→4)
ne ... jamais personne	(→5)
ne ... jamais rien	(→6)
ne ... jamais que	(→7)
ne ... jamais ni ... ni ...	(→8)
(ne ... pas) non plus	(→9)

non and **pas**

- **non** *no* is the usual negative response to a question (→10)
  It is often translated as *not* (→11)
- **pas** is generally used when a distinction is being made, or for emphasis (→12)
  It is often translated as *not* (→13)

1 **Je ne le ferai plus jamais**
I'll never do it again

2 **Je ne connais plus personne à Rouen**
I don't know anybody in Rouen any more

3 **Les marchandises ne valaient plus rien**
The goods were no longer worth anything

4 **Il n'avait plus ni femme ni enfants**
He no longer had either a wife or children

5 **On n'y voit jamais personne**
You never see anybody there

6 **Elle n'a jamais rien changé**
She has never changed anything

7 **Je n'ai jamais parlé qu'à sa femme**
I've only ever spoken to his wife

8 **Il ne m'a jamais ni écrit ni téléphoné**
He has never either written to me or phoned me

9 **Ils n'ont pas d'enfants et nous non plus**
They don't have any children and neither do we
Je ne les aime pas – Moi non plus
I don't like them – Neither do I, I don't either

10 **Vous voulez nous accompagner? – Non**
Do you want to come with us? – No (I don't)

11 **Tu viens ou non?**
Are you coming or not?
J'espère que non
I hope not

12 **Ma sœur aime le ski, moi pas**
My sister likes skiing, I don't

13 **Qui l'a fait? – Pas moi!**
Who did it? – Not me!
Est-il de retour? – Pas encore
Is he back? – Not yet
Tu as froid? – Pas du tout
Are you cold? – Not at all

Question forms: direct

There are four ways of forming direct questions in French:

- by inverting the normal word order so that
  pronoun subject + verb → verb + pronoun subject.
  A hyphen links the verb and pronoun (→**1**)

  - When the subject is a noun, a pronoun is inserted after the verb and linked to it by a hyphen (→**2**)
  - When the verb ends in a vowel in the third person singular, **-t-** is inserted before the pronoun (→**3**)

- by maintaining the word order *subject + verb*, but by using a rising intonation at the end of the sentence (→**4**)

- by inserting **est-ce que** before the construction *subject + verb* (→**5**)

- by using an interrogative word at the beginning of the sentence, together with inversion *or* the **est-ce que** form above (→**6**)

1 Aimez-vous la France?
Do you like France?
Est-ce possible?
Is it possible?
Part-on tout de suite?
Are we leaving right away?

Avez-vous fini?
Have you finished?
Est-elle restée?
Did she stay?

2 Tes parents sont-ils heureux?
Are your parents happy?
Simon est-il parti?
Has Simon left?

3 A-t-elle de l'argent?
Has she any money?
La pièce dure-t-elle longtemps?
Does the play last long?
Mon père a-t-il téléphoné?
Has my father phoned?

4 Il l'a fini
He's finished it
Paul va venir
Paul's coming

Il l'a fini?
Has he finished it?
Paul va venir?
Is Paul coming?

5 Est-ce que tu la connais?
Do you know her?
Est-ce que tes parents sont revenus d'Italie?
Have your parents come back from Italy?

6 Quel train ⸨prends-tu?
       ⸨est-ce que tu prends?**
What train are you getting?
Lequel ⸨est-ce que ta sœur préfère?
        ⸨ta sœur préfère-t-elle?**
Which one does your sister prefer?
Quand ⸨êtes-vous arrivé?
       ⸨est-ce que vous êtes arrivé?**
When did you arrive?
Pourquoi ⸨ne sont-ils pas venus?
         ⸨est-ce qu'ils ne sont pas venus?**
Why haven't they come?

Question forms: indirect

An indirect question is one that is 'reported', e.g. he asked me *what the time was*, tell me *which way to go*. Word order in indirect questions is as follows:

- *interrogative word* + *subject* + *verb* (→1)
- when the subject is a noun, and not a pronoun, the subject and verb are often inverted (→2)

n'est-ce pas

This is used wherever English would use *isn't it?*, *don't they?*, *weren't we?*, *is it?* etc. tagged on to the end of a sentence (→3)

oui and si

Oui is the word for *yes* in answer to a question put in the affirmative (→4)

Si is the word for *yes* in answer to a question put in the negative or to contradict a negative statement (→5)

1 **Je me demande s'il viendra**
I wonder if he'll come
Je ne sais pas à quoi ça sert
I don't know what it's for
Dites-moi quel autobus va à la gare
Tell me which bus goes to the station
Il m'a demandé combien d'argent j'avais
He asked me how much money I had

2 **Elle ne sait pas à quelle heure commence le film**
She doesn't know what time the film starts
Je me demande où sont tes gants
I wonder where your gloves are
Elle nous a demandé comment allait notre père
She asked us how our father was
Je ne sais pas ce que veulent dire ces mots
I don't know what these words mean

3 **Il fait chaud, n'est-ce pas?**
It's warm, isn't it?
Vous n'oublierez pas, n'est-ce pas?
You won't forget, will you?

4 **Tu l'as fait? – Oui**
Have you done it? – Yes (I have)

5 **Tu ne l'as pas fait? – Si**
Haven't you done it? – Yes (I have)

Numbers

Cardinal (*one, two etc.*)		**Ordinal** (*first, second etc.*)	
zéro	0		
un (une)	1	premier (première)	1er, 1ère
deux	2	deuxième, second(e)	2ème
trois	3	troisième	3ème
quatre	4	quatrième	4ème
cinq	5	cinquième	5ème
six	6	sixième	6ème
sept	7	septième	7ème
huit	8	huitième	8ème
neuf	9	neuvième	9ème
dix	10	dixième	10ème
onze	11	onzième	11ème
douze	12	douzième	12ème
treize	13	treizième	13ème
quatorze	14	quatorzième	14ème
quinze	15	quinzième	15ème
seize	16	seizième	16ème
dix-sept	17	dix-septième	17ème
dix-huit	18	dix-huitième	18ème
dix-neuf	19	dix-neuvième	19ème
vingt	20	vingtième	20ème
vingt et un (une)	21	vingt et unième	21ème
vingt-deux	22	vingt-deuxième	22ème
vingt-trois	23	vingt-troisième	23ème
trente	30	trentième	30ème
quarante	40	quarantième	40ème
cinquante	50	cinquantième	50ème
soixante	60	soixantième	60ème
soixante-dix	70	soixante-dixième	70ème
soixante et onze	71	soixante-onzième	71ème
soixante-douze	72	soixante-douzième	72ème
quatre-vingts	80	quatre-vingtième	80ème
quatre-vingt-un (une)	81	quatre-vingt-unième	81ème
quatre-vingt-dix	90	quatre-vingt-dixième	90ème
quatre-vingt-onze	91	quatre-vingt-onzième	91ème

Numbers (ctd.)

Cardinal		Ordinal	
cent	100	centième	100ème
cent un (une)	101	cent unième	101ème
cent deux	102	cent deuxième	102ème
cent dix	110	cent dixième	110ème
cent quarante-deux	142	cent quarante-deuxième	142ème
deux cents	200	deux centième	200ème
deux cent un (une)	201	deux cent unième	201ème
deux cent deux	202	deux cent-deuxième	202ème
trois cents	300	trois centième	300ème
quatre cents	400	quatre centième	400ème
cinq cents	500	cinq centième	500ème
six cents	600	six centième	600ème
sept cents	700	sept centième	700ème
huit cents	800	huit centième	800ème
neuf cents	900	neuf centième	900ème
mille	1000	millième	1000ème
mille un (une)	1001	mille unième	1001ème
mille deux	1002	mille deuxième	1002ème
deux mille	2000	deux millième	2000ème
cent mille	100.000	cent millième	100.000ème
un million	1.000.000	millionième	1.000.000ème
deux millions	2.000.000	deux millionième	2.000.000ème

Fractions		Others	
un demi, une demie	½	zéro virgule cinq	0,5
un tiers	⅓	un virgule trois	1,3
deux tiers	⅔	dix pour cent	10%
un quart	¼	deux plus deux	2 + 2
trois quarts	¾	deux moins deux	2 − 2
un cinquième	⅕	deux fois deux	2 × 2
cinq et trois quarts	5¾	deux divisé par deux	2 ÷ 2

Note the use of points with large numbers and commas with fractions, i.e. the opposite of English usage.

Numbers: Other Uses

- -aine denoting approximate numbers:

une douzaine (de pommes)	about a dozen (apples)
une quinzaine (d'hommes)	about fifteen (men)
des centaines de personnes	hundreds of people
BUT: **un millier (d'autos)**	about a thousand (cars)

- measurements:

vingt mètres carrés	20 square metres
vingt mètres cubes	20 cubic metres
un pont long de quarante mètres	a bridge 40 metres long
avoir trois mètres de large/de haut	to be 3 metres wide/high

- miscellaneous:

Il habite au dix	He lives at number 10
C'est au chapitre sept	It's in chapter 7
(C'est) à la page 17	(It's) on page 17
(Il habite) au septième étage	(He lives) on the 7th floor
Il est arrivé le septième	He came in 7th
une part d'un septième	a share of one seventh
échelle au vingt-cinq millième	scale 1:25,000

Telephone numbers

J'aimerais Paris trois cent trente-quatre, vingt-deux, dix
I would like Paris 334 22 10

Pouvez-vous m'appeler Dijon vingt-deux, zéro huit, trente
Could you get me Dijon 22 08 30

Poste trois cent trente-cinq
Extension number 335

Poste vingt-deux, trente-trois
Extension number 22 33

N.B. In French, telephone numbers are broken down into two sets of
two numbers, and are not spoken separately as in English. They are
also written in groups of two or three numbers (never four).

The calendar

Dates

Quelle est la date aujourd'hui?	
Quel jour sommes-nous?	What's the date today?

C'est ...	
Nous sommes ...	It's the ...
le premier février	1st of February
le deux février	2nd of February
le vingt-huit février	28th of February

Il vient le sept mars   He's coming on the 7th of March

N.B. Use cardinal numbers except for the first of the month.

Years

Je suis né en 1949
I was born in 1949

le douze février	**dix-neuf cent quarante-neuf**
	mil neuf cent quarante-neuf

(on) 12th February 1949

N.B. There are two ways of expressing the year (see last example).
Note the spelling of **mil** *one thousand* in dates

Other expressions

dans les années cinquante	during the fifties
au vingtième siècle	in the twentieth century
en mai	in May
lundi (quinze)	on Monday (the 15th)
le lundi	on Mondays
dans dix jours	in 10 days' time
il y a dix jours	10 days ago

The Time

Quelle heure est-il?	*What time is it?*
Il est ...	*It's ...*

00.00	**minuit** *midnight, twelve o'clock*
00.10	**minuit dix**
00.15	**minuit et quart**
00.30	**minuit et demie, minuit trente**
00.45	**une heure moins (le) quart**
01.00	**une heure du matin** *one a.m., one o'clock in the morning*
01.10	**une heure dix (du matin)**
01.15	**une heure et quart, une heure quinze**
01.30	**une heure et demie, une heure trente**
01.45	**deux heures moins (le) quart, une heure quarante-cinq, une heure trois quarts**
01.50	**deux heures moins dix, une heure cinquante**
01.59	**deux heures moins une, une heure cinquante-neuf**
12.00	**midi, douze heures** *noon, twelve o'clock*
12.30	**midi et demie, midi trente**
13.00	**une heure de l'après-midi, treize heures** *one p.m., one o'clock in the afternoon*
01.30	**une heure et demie (de l'après-midi), une heure trente, treize heures trente**
19.00	**sept heures du soir, dix-neuf heures** *seven p.m., seven o'clock in the evening*
19.30	**sept heures et demie (du soir), sept heures trente, dix-neuf heures trente**

A quelle heure venez-vous? – A sept heures
What time are you coming? – At seven o'clock
Les bureaux sont fermés de midi à quatorze heures
The offices are closed from twelve until two
à deux heures du matin/de l'après-midi
at two o'clock in the morning/afternoon, at two a.m./p.m.
à sept heures du soir
at seven o'clock in the evening, at seven p.m.
à cinq heures précises or **pile**
at five o'clock sharp
vers neuf heures
about nine o'clock
peu avant/après midi
shortly before/after noon
entre huit et neuf heures
between eight and nine o'clock
Il est plus de trois heures et demie
It's after half past three
Il faut y être à dix heures au plus tard/au plus tôt
You have to be there by ten o'clock at the latest/earliest
Ne venez pas plus tard que onze heures moins le quart
Come no later than a quarter to eleven
Il en a pour une demi-heure
He'll be half an hour (at it)
Elle est restée sans connaissance pendant un quart d'heure
She was unconscious for a quarter of an hour
Je les attends depuis une heure
I've been waiting for them for an hour/since one o'clock
Ils sont partis il y a quelques minutes
They left a few minutes ago
Je l'ai fait en vingt minutes
I did it in twenty minutes
Le train arrive dans une heure
The train arrives in an hour('s time)
Combien de temps dure la pièce?
How long does the play last?

Beware of translating word for word. While on occasion this is quite possible, quite often it is not. The need for caution is illustrated by the following:

- English phrasal verbs (i.e. verbs followed by a preposition) e.g. *to run away*, *to fall down* are often translated by one word in French (→**1**)

- English verbal constructions often contain a preposition where none exists in French, or vice versa (→**2**)

- Two or more prepositions in English may have a single rendering in French (→**3**)

- A word which is singular in English may be plural in French, or vice versa (→**4**)

- French has no equivalent of the possessive construction denoted by --'s/--s' (→**5**)
  See also *at/in/to*, p. 234

Specific problems

-ing

This is translated in a variety of ways in French:

- *to be* ...*-ing* is translated by a simple verb (→**6**)
  Exception: when a physical position is denoted, a past participle is used (→**7**)

- in the construction *to see/hear sb* ...*-ing*, use an infinitive or **qui** + verb (→**8**)

-ing can also be translated by:
  - an infinitive (→**9**)
    (see p. 44)
  - a perfect infinitive (→**10**)
    (see p. 46)
  - a present participle (→**11**)
    (see p. 48)
  - a noun (→**12**)

Continued

1 **s'enfuir**   **tomber**   **céder**
       to run away   to fall down   to give in

2 **payer**   **regarder**   **écouter**
       to pay for   to look at   to listen to
       obéir à   **nuire à**   **manquer de**
       to obey   to harm   to lack

3 **s'étonner de**   **satisfait de**
       to be surprised at   satisfied with
       voler qch à   **apte à**
       to steal sth from   capable of; fit for

4 **les bagages**   **ses cheveux**
       the luggage   his/her hair
       le bétail   **mon pantalon**
       the cattle   my trousers

5 **l'auto de mon frère**   **la chambre des enfants**
       my brother's car   the children's bedroom
       (*literally: ... of my brother*)   (*literally: ... of the children*)

6 **Il part demain**   **Je lisais un roman**
       He's leaving tomorrow   I was reading a novel

7 **Elle est assise là-bas**   **Il était couché par terre**
       She is sitting over there   He was lying on the ground

8 Je les vois $\left\{\begin{array}{l}\textbf{venir}\\ \textbf{qui viennent}\end{array}\right\}$ I can see them coming

       Je l'ai entendue $\left\{\begin{array}{l}\textbf{chanter}\\ \textbf{qui chantait}\end{array}\right\}$ I heard her singing

9 **J'aime aller au cinéma**   **Arrêtez de parler!**
       I like going to the cinema   Stop talking!
       Au lieu de répondre   **Avant de partir**
       Instead of answering   Before leaving

10 **Après avoir ouvert la boîte, il ...**
       After opening the box, he ...

11 **Etant plus timide que moi, elle ...**
       Being shyer than me, she ...

12 **Le ski me maintient en forme**
       Skiing keeps me fit

to be

- Generally translated by **être** (→1)
  When physical location is implied, **se trouver** may be used (→2)

- In set expressions, describing physical and emotional conditions, **avoir** is used:

  avoir chaud/froid   *to be warm/cold*
  avoir faim/soif   *to be hungry/thirsty*
  avoir peur/honte   *to be afraid/ashamed*
  avoir tort/raison   *to be wrong/right*

- Describing the weather, e.g. *what's the weather like?*, *it's windy/sunny*, use **faire** (→3)

- For ages, e.g. *he is 6*, use **avoir** (→4)

- For state of health, e.g. *he's unwell, how are you?*, use **aller** (→5)

it is, it's

- Usually **il/elle est**, when referring to a noun (→6)

- For expressions of time, also use **il est** (→7)

- To describe the weather, e.g. *it's windy*, see above

- In the construction: *it is difficult/easy to do sth*, use **il est** (→8)

- In all other constructions, use **c'est** (→9)

there is/there are

- Both are translated by **il y a** (→10)

can, be able

- Physical ability is expressed by **pouvoir** (→11)

- If the meaning is *to know how to*, use **savoir** (→12)

- *Can* + a 'verb of hearing or seeing etc.' in English is not translated in French (→13)

1 **Il est tard**
It's late

   C'est peu probable
It's not very likely

2 **Où se trouve la gare?**
Where's the station?

3 **Quel temps fait-il?**
What's the weather like?

   Il fait beau/mauvais/du vent
It's lovely/miserable/windy

4 **Quel âge avez-vous?**
How old are you?

   J'ai quinze ans
I'm fifteen

5 **Comment allez-vous?**
How are you?

   Je vais très bien
I'm very well

6 **Où est mon parapluie? – Il est là, dans le coin**
Where's my umbrella? – It's there, in the corner

   Descends la valise si elle n'est pas trop lourde
Bring down the case if it isn't too heavy

7 **Quelle heure est-il? – Il est sept heures et demie**
What's the time? – It's half past seven

8 **Il est difficile de répondre à cette question**
It's difficult to reply to this question

9 **C'est moi qui ne l'aime pas**
It's me who doesn't like him

   C'est Paul/ma mère qui l'a dit
It's Paul/my mother who said so

   C'est ici que je les ai achetés
It's here that I bought them

   C'est parce que ma mère est malade que …
It's because my mother is ill that …

10 **Il y a un monsieur à la porte**
There's a gentleman at the door

   Il y a cinq livres sur la table
There are five books on the table

11 **Pouvez-vous atteindre cette étagère?**
Can you reach up to that shelf?

12 **Elle ne sait pas nager**
She can't swim

13 **Je ne vois rien**
I can't see anything

   Il les entendait
He could hear them

to (see also below)

- Generally translated by **à** (→1)
  (See p. 204)

- In time expressions, e.g *10 to 6*, use **moins** (→2)

- When the meaning is *in order to*, use **pour** (→3)

- Following a verb, as in *to try to do*, *to like to do*, see pp. 44 and 64

- *easy/difficult/impossible* etc. *to do*:
  The preposition used depends on whether a specific noun is
  referred to (→4) or not (→5)

at/in/to

- With feminine countries, use **en** (→6)
  With masculine countries, use **au** (**aux** with plural countries)
  (→7)

- With towns, use **à** (→8)

- *at/to the butcher's/grocer's* etc.: use **à** + noun designating the
  shop, or **chez** + noun designating the shopkeeper (→9)

- *at/to the dentist's/doctor's* etc.: use **chez** (→10)

- *at/to ...'s/ ...s' house*: use **chez** (→11)

1 **Donne le livre à Corinne**
   Give the book to Corinne

2 **dix heures moins cinq** **à sept heures moins le quart**
   five to ten   at a quarter to seven

3 **Je l'ai fait pour vous aider**
   I did it to help you
   Il se pencha pour nouer son lacet
   He bent down to tie his shoelace

4 **Ce livre est difficile à lire**
   This book is difficult to read

5 **Il est difficile de comprendre leurs raisons**
   It's difficult to understand their reasons

6 **Il est allé en France/en Suisse**
   He has gone to France/to Switzerland
   un village en Norvège/en Belgique
   a village in Norway/in Belgium

7 **Etes-vous allé au Canada/au Danemark/aux Etats-Unis?**
   Have you been to Canada/to Denmark/to the United States?
   une ville au Japon/au Brésil
   a town in Japan/in Brazil

8 **Il est allé à Vienne/à Bruxelles**
   He has gone to Vienna/to Brussels
   Il habite à Londres/à Genève
   He lives in London/in Geneva
   Ils logent dans un hôtel à St. Pierre
   They're staying in a hotel at St. Pierre

9 **Je l'ai acheté** { **à l'épicerie** I bought it at the grocer's
        { **chez l'épicier**
   Elle est allée { **à la boulangerie**
        { **chez le boulanger** She's gone to the baker's

10 **J'ai un rendez-vous chez le dentiste**
   I've an appointment at the dentist's
   Il est allé chez le médecin
   He has gone to the doctor's

11 **chez Claude**   **chez les Courtin**
   at/to Claude's house at/to the Courtins' house

General Points

- Activity of the lips
  The lips play a very important part in French. When a vowel is
  described as having 'rounded' lips, the lips are slightly drawn
  together and pursed, as when an English speaker expresses
  exaggerated surprise with the vowel 'ooh!'. Equally, if the lips are
  said to be 'spread', the corners are pulled firmly back towards the
  cheeks, tending to reveal the front teeth.
  In English, lip position is not important, and vowel sounds tend
  to merge because of this. In French, the activity of the lips means
  that every vowel sound is clearly distinct from every other.

- No diphthongs
  A diphthong is a glide between two vowel sounds in the same
  syllable. In English, there are few 'pure' vowel sounds, but
  largely diphthongs instead. Although speakers of English may
  think they produce one vowel sound in the word 'day', in fact they
  use a diphthong, which in this instance is a glide between the
  vowels [e] and [ɪ]: [deɪ]. In French the tension maintained in the
  lips, tongue and the mouth in general prevents diphthongs
  occurring, as the vowel sound is kept constant throughout. Hence
  the French word corresponding to the above example, 'dé', is
  pronounced with no final [ɪ] sound, but is phonetically
  represented thus: [de].

- Consonants
  In English, consonants are often pronounced with a degree of
  laxness that can result in their practically disappearing altogether
  although not strictly 'silent'. In a relaxed pronunciation of a word
  such as 'hat', the 't' is often scarcely heard, or is replaced by a
  'glottal stop' (a sort of jerk in the throat). This never occurs in
  French, where consonants are always given their full value.

Pronunciation of Consonants

Some consonants are pronounced almost exactly as in English:
[b, p, f, v, g, k, m, w].
Most others are similar to English, but slight differences should be
noted.

EXAMPLES	HINTS ON PRONUNCIATION
[d] **d**in**d**e	
[t] **t**en**t**e	The tip of the tongue touches the upper front teeth and not the roof of the mouth as in English
[n] **n**o**nn**e	
[l] Li**ll**e	
[s] tou**s ç**a	The tip of the tongue is down behind the bottom front teeth, lower than in English
[z] **z**éro ro**s**e	
[ʃ] **ch**ose ta**ch**e	Like the *sh* of English *shout*
[ʒ] **j**e **g**ilet bei**g**e	Like the *s* of English *measure*
[j] **y**eux pai**ll**e	Like the *y* of English *yes*

Three consonants are not heard in English:

[ʀ] **r**a**r**e veni**r**	*R* is often silent in English, e.g. fa*r*m. In French the [ʀ] is never silent, unless it follows an **e** at the end of a word e.g. cherche**r**. To pronounce it, try to make a short sound like gargling. Similar, too, to the Scottish pronunciation of lo*ch*.
[ɲ] vi**gn**e a**gn**eau	Similar to the *ni* of Spa*ni*ard
[ɥ] h**u**ile l**u**eur	Like a very rapid [y] (see p. 239) followed immediately by the next vowel of the word

Pronunciation of Vowels

EXAMPLES	HINTS ON PRONUNCIATION
[a] patte plat amour	Similar to the vowel in English *pat*
[ɑ] bas pâte	Longer than the sound above, it resembles the English exclamation of surprise *ah!* Similar, too, to the English vowel in *car* without the final *r* sound
[ɛ] lait jouet merci	Similar to the English vowel in *pet*. Beware of using the English diphthong [eɪ] as in *pay*
[e] été jouer	A pure vowel, again quite different from the diphthong in English *pay*
[ə] le premier	Similar to the English sound in but*ter* when the *r* is not pronounced
[i] ici vie lycée	The lips are well spread towards the cheeks while uttering this sound. Shorter than the English vowel in *see*
[ɔ] mort homme	The lips are well rounded while producing a sound similar to the *o* of English *cot*
[o] mot dôme eau	A pure vowel with strongly rounded lips; quite different from the diphthong in English *bone, low*

[u] **genou roue**	A pure vowel with strongly rounded lips. Similar to the English *ooh!* of surprise
[y] **rue vêtu**	Often the most difficult for English speakers to produce: round your lips and try to pronounce [i] (see above). There is no [j] sound (see p. 237) as there is in English *pure*
[œ] **sœur beurre**	Similar to the vowel in English *fir* or *murmur*, but without the *r* sound and with the lips more strongly rounded
[ø] **peu deux**	To pronounce this, try to say [e] (see above) with the lips strongly rounded

Nasal Vowels

These are spelt with a vowel followed by a 'nasal' consonant – **n** or **m**. The production of nasal vowels really requires the help of a teacher or a recording of the sound. However, to help you, the vowel is pronounced by allowing the air from the lungs to come partly down the nose and partly through the mouth, and the **n** or **m** is not pronounced at all.

[ã] **lent sang dans**	
[ɛ̃] **matin plein**	In each case, the vowel shown in the phonetic symbol is pronounced as described above, but air is allowed to come through the nose as well as the mouth
[ɔ̃] **non pont**	
[œ̃] **brun un parfum**	

From Spelling to Sounds

Although it may not seem so at first sight, there are some fairly precise 'rules' which can help you to know how to pronounce French words from their spelling.

Vowels

SPELLING	PRONOUNCED	EXAMPLES
a, à	[a]	chatte, table
a, â	[ɑ]	pâte, pas
e, é	[e]	été, marcher
e, è, ê	[ɛ]	fenêtre, fermer, chère
e	[ə]	double, fenêtre
i, î, y	[i]	lit, abîmer, lycée
o, ô	[o]	pot, trop, dôme
o	[ɔ]	sotte, orange
u, û	[y]	battu, fût, pur

Vowel Groups

There are several groups of vowels in French spelling which are regularly pronounced in the same way:

ai	[ɛ] or [e]	maison, marchai, faire
ail	[aj]	portail
ain, aim, (e)in, im	[ɛ̃]	pain, faim, frein, impair
au	[o]	auberge, landau
an, am, en, em	[ɑ̃]	plan, ample, entrer, temps
eau	[o]	bateau, eau
eu	[œ] or [ø]	feu, peur
euil(le), ueil	[œj]	feuille, recueil
oi, oy	[wa]	voire, voyage
on, om	[ɔ̃]	ton, compter
ou	[u]	hibou, outil
œu	[œ]	sœur, cœur
ue	[y]	rue
un, um	[œ̃]	brun, parfum

Added to these are the many groups of letters occurring at the end of words, where their pronunciation is predictable, bearing in mind the tendency (see p. 242) of final consonants to remain silent:

TYPICAL WORDS	PRONUNCIATION OF FINAL SYLLABLE
pas, mât, chat	[ɑ] or [a]
marcher, marchez, marchais, marchait, baie, valet, mes, fumée	[e] or [ɛ]
nid	[i]
chaud, vaut, faux, sot, tôt, Pernod, dos, croc	[o]
bout, bijoux, sous, boue	[u]
fut, fût, crus, crûs	[y]
queue, heureux, bleus	[ø]
en, vend, vent, an, sang, grand, dans	[ã]
fin, feint, frein, vain	[ɛ̃]
on, pont, fond, avons	[ɔ̃]
brun, parfum	[œ̃]

Continued

From Spelling to Sounds (ctd.)

Consonants

- Final consonants are usually silent (→**1**)

- **n** or **m** at the end of a syllable or word are silent, but they have the effect of 'nasalizing' the preceding vowel(s) (see p. 239 on Nasal Vowels)

- The letter **h** is either 'silent' ('mute') or 'aspirate' when it begins a word. When silent, the word behaves as though it started with a vowel and takes a liaison with the preceding word where appropriate.
  When the **h** is aspirate, no liaison is made (→**2**)
  There is no way of predicting which words start with which sort of **h** – this simply has to be learnt with each word

- The following consonants in spelling have predictable pronunciations: b, d, f, k, l, p, r, t, v, w, x, y, z. Others vary:

SPELLING	PRONOUNCED	ENGLISH EXAMPLES	
c + a, o, u	[k]	*can, cot, cut*	(→**3**)
+ l, r		*class, cram*	
c + e, i, y	[s]	*ceiling, ice*	(→**4**)
ç + a, o, u	[s]	*ceiling, ice*	(→**5**)
ch	[ʃ]	*shop, lash*	(→**6**)
g + a, o, u	[g]	*gate, got, gun*	(→**7**)
+ l, r		*glass, gramme*	
g + e, i, y	[ʒ]	*leisure*	(→**8**)
gn	[n]	*compa*n*ion, o*n*ion*	(→**9**)
j	[ʒ]	*measure*	(→**10**)
q, qu	[k]	*quay, kit*	(→**11**)
s between vowels:	[z]	*rose*	(→**12**)
elsewhere:	[s]	*sit*	
th	[t]	*Thomas*	(→**13**)
t in **-tion**	[s]	*sit*	(→**14**)

1	éclat	nez	
	[ekla]	[ne]	
	chaud	aider	
	[ʃo]	[ede]	
2	silent h:	aspirate h:	
	des hôtels	des haricots	
	[de zotel]	[de aRiko]	
3	café	côte	culotte
	[kafe]	[kot]	[kylɔt]
	classe	croûte	
	[klas]	[kRut]	
4	ceci	cil	cycliste
	[səsi]	[sil]	[siklist]
5	ça	arçon	déçu
	[sɑ]	[aRsɔ̃]	[desy]
6	chat	riche	
	[ʃa]	[Riʃ]	
7	gare	gourde	aigu
	[gaR]	[guRd]	[εgy]
	glaise	gramme	
	[glεz]	[gRam]	
8	gemme	gilet	gymnaste
	[ʒεm]	[ʒilε]	[ʒimnast]
9	vigne	oignon	
	[viɲ]	[ɔɲɔ̃]	
0	joli	Jules	
	[ʒɔli]	[ʒyl]	
1	coq	quitter	
	[kɔk]	[kite]	
2	sable	maison	
	[sablə]	[mezɔ̃]	
3	théâtre	Thomas	
	[teɑtR]	[tɔma]	
4	nation	action	
	[nasjɔ̃]	[aksjɔ̃]	

Feminine Forms and Pronunciation

- For adjectives and nouns ending in a vowel in the masculine, the addition of an **e** to form the feminine does not alter the pronunciation (→1)

- If the masculine ends with a silent consonant, generally -d, -s, -x or -t, the consonant is sounded in the feminine (→2)
  This also applies when the final consonant is doubled before the addition of the feminine **e** (→3)

- If the masculine ends in a nasal vowel and a silent **n**, e.g. -an, -on, -in, the vowel is no longer nasalized and the -n is pronounced in the feminine (→4)
  This also applies when the final -n is doubled before the addition of the feminine **e** (→5)

- Where the masculine and feminine forms have totally different endings (see pp. 136 and 150), the pronunciation of course varies accordingly (→6)

Plural Forms and Pronunciation

- The addition of s or x to form regular plurals generally does not affect pronunciation (→7)

- Where liaison has to be made, the final -s or -x of the plural form is pronounced (→8)

- Where the masculine singular and plural forms have totally different endings (see pp. 138 and 148), the pronunciation of course varies accordingly (→9)

- Note the change in pronunciation in the following nouns:

SINGULAR		PLURAL		
bœuf	[bœf]	bœufs	[bø]	ox/oxen
œuf	[œf]	œufs	[ø]	egg/eggs
os	[ɔs]	os	[o]	bone/bones

ADJECTIVES		NOUNS	
1 joli	→ jolie	un ami	→ une amie
[ʒɔli]	[ʒɔli]	[ami]	[ami]
déçu	→ déçue	un employé	→ une employée
[desy]	[desy]	[ãplwaje]	[ãplwaje]
2 chaud	→ chaude	un idiot	→ une idiote
[ʃo]	[ʃod]	[idjo]	[idjɔt]
français	→ française	un Anglais	→ une Anglaise
[fʀãsɛ]	[fʀãsɛz]	[ãglɛ]	[ãglɛz]
inquiet	→ inquiète	un étranger	→ une étrangère
[ɛ̃kjɛ]	[ɛ̃kjɛt]	[etʀãʒe]	[etʀãʒɛʀ]
3 violet	→ violette	le cadet	→ la cadette
[vjɔlɛ]	[vjɔlɛt]	[kadɛ]	[kadɛt]
gras	→ grasse		
[gʀɑ]	[gʀɑs]		
4 plein	→ pleine	le souverain	→ la souveraine
[plɛ̃]	[plɛn]	[suvʀɛ̃]	[suvʀɛn]
fin	→ fine	le Persan	→ la Persane
[fɛ̃]	[fin]	[pɛʀsã]	[pɛʀsan]
brun	→ brune	le voisin	→ la voisine
[bʀœ̃]	[bʀyn]	[vwazɛ̃]	[vwazin]
5 canadien	→ canadienne	le paysan	→ la paysanne
[kanadjɛ̃]	[kanadjɛn]	[peizã]	[peizan]
breton	→ bretonne	le baron	→ la baronne
[bʀətɔ̃]	[bʀətɔn]	[baʀɔ̃]	[baʀɔn]
6 juif	→ juive	le veuf	→ la veuve
[ʒɥif]	[ʒɥiv]	[vœf]	[vœv]
traître	→ traîtresse	le maître	→ la maîtresse
[tʀɛtʀə]	[tʀɛtʀɛs]	[mɛtʀə]	[mɛtʀɛs]
7 beau	→ beaux	la maison	→ les maisons
[bo]	[bo]	[mɛzɔ̃]	[mɛzɔ̃]
8 des anciens élèves			
[de zãsjɛ̃ zelɛv]			
de beaux habits			
[də bo zabi]			
9 brutal	→ brutaux	un journal	→ des journaux
[bʀytal]	[bʀyto]	[ʒuʀnal]	[ʒuʀno]

The Alphabet

A, a	[ɑ]	J, j	[ʒi]	S, s	[ɛs]
B, b	[be]	K, k	[ka]	T, t	[te]
C, c	[se]	L, l	[ɛl]	U, u	[y]
D, d	[de]	M, m	[ɛm]	V, v	[ve]
E, e	[ə]	N, n	[ɛn]	W, w	[dubləve]
F, f	[ɛf]	O, o	[o]	X, x	[iks]
G, g	[ʒe]	P, p	[pe]	Y, y	[igrɛk]
H, h	[aʃ]	Q, q	[ky]	Z, z	[zɛd]
I, i	[i]	R, r	[ɛʀ]		

Capital letters are used as in English *except* for the following:

- adjectives of nationality
  e.g. **une ville espagnole**   **un auteur français**
  a Spanish town   a French author

- languages
  e.g. **Parlez-vous anglais?**   **Il parle français et allemand**
  Do you speak English?   He speaks French and German

- days of the week:
  lundi Monday
  mardi Tuesday
  mercredi Wednesday
  jeudi Thursday
  vendredi Friday
  samedi Saturday
  dimanche Sunday

- months of the year:

janvier	January	**juillet**	July
février	February	**août**	August
mars	March	**septembre**	September
avril	April	**octobre**	October
mai	May	**novembre**	November
juin	June	**décembre**	December

INDEX **247**

The following index lists comprehensively both grammatical terms and key words in French and English contained in this book.

COLLINS BILINGUAL GEM DICTIONARIES

A wealth of language information in a handy pocket-size volume, with all the well-known features of Collins bilingual dictionaries:

- more entries than any other comparable dictionary
- thousands of current phrases and constructions
- meanings and usage clearly indicated

Titles include:

COLLINS GEM FRENCH DICTIONARY	ISBN 0-00-458539-9
COLLINS GEM GERMAN DICTIONARY	ISBN 0-00-458926-2
COLLINS GEM GREEK DICTIONARY	ISBN 0-00-458548-8
COLLINS GEM ITALIAN DICTIONARY	ISBN 0-00-458546-1
COLLINS GEM PORTUGUESE DICTIONARY	ISBN 0-00-458666-2
COLLINS GEM SPANISH DICTIONARY	ISBN 0-00-458544-5

ALSO AVAILABLE IN THE GEM LANGUAGE STUDY SERIES

COLLINS GEM 5000 FRENCH WORDS	ISBN 0-00-459323-5
COLLINS GEM FRENCH VERB TABLES	ISBN 0-00-459305-7
COLLINS GEM 5000 GERMAN WORDS	ISBN 0-00-459322-7
COLLINS GEM GERMAN GRAMMAR	ISBN 0-00-459335-9
COLLINS GEM GERMAN VERB TABLES	ISBN 0-00-459339-1
COLLINS GEM SPANISH VERB TABLES AND GRAMMAR	ISBN 0-00-459340-5